THE BEGIN...

broadband

AND wireless INTERNET

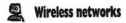 Wireless networks

 Computer security

Instant messaging

Downloading music

PC phone calls

Wi-Fi and laptops

PETER BURNS

summersdale

THE BEGINNER'S GUIDE TO BROADBAND AND
WIRELESS INTERNET
Copyright © Peter Burns, 2006

Microsoft ® and Windows ® are registered trademarks of
Microsoft Corporation. All other trademarks are acknowledged
as belonging to their respective companies.

The right of Peter Burns to be identified as the author of this
work has been asserted in accordance with sections 77 and 78 of
the Copyright, Designs and Patents Act 1988.

Summersdale Publishers Ltd
46 West Street
Chichester
West Sussex
PO19 1RP
UK

www.summersdale.com

Printed and bound in Great Britain

ISBN: 1-84024-499-2
ISBN: 978-1-84024-499-1

Warning and Disclaimer

Every effort has been made to make this book as accurate as possible. The author and publishers shall have neither responsibility nor liability to any person or entity with respect to any loss or damage arising from information contained within this book.

Every effort has been made to obtain the necessary permissions with reference to copyright material, both illustrative and quoted; should there be any omissions in this respect, we apologise and shall be pleased to make the appropriate acknowledgements in any future edition.

Acknowledgements

All screenshots and images reprinted by kind permission.
AVG Anti-Virus screenshot copyright © Grisoft Inc.
BBC News Player screenshot copyright © British Broadcasting Corporation courtesy of bbc.co.uk/news.
Blinkx TV screenshots copyright © blinkx.
Screenshots of BT websites and BT OpenZone Access Manager copyright © British Telecommunications plc.
Bulent's Screen Recorder screenshots copyright © and used by permission of Bulent Baltacioglu.
Clipshack screenshots copyright © Reality Digital Inc.
ZDNet UK screenshot originally appeared on the CNET website and is copyright © 2005 CNET Networks, Inc. All rights reserved. ZDNET UK is a registered service mark of CNET Networks, Inc. ZDNET Logo is a service mark of CNET NETWORKS, Inc.
MicroLink image copyright © devolo AG.
Dropload screenshot copyright © Dropload.
Flickr screenshots copyright Yahoo! Inc.
iMesh screenshots copyright © iMesh.
JiWire screenshot copyright © JiWire Inc.

Thanks to Gillian at Summersdale and a special thanks to
my wife Anna, who helped make this book possible.

Contents

Chapter Six:
Downloading Music...**82**

Chapter Seven:
TV, Video and Webcams...**106**

Chapter Eight:
PC Phone Calls...**127**

Chapter Nine:
E-mail and Digital Photography.............................148

Chapter Ten:
Wireless at Home..164

Introduction

Broadband has made the Internet a much more exciting place to visit and revolutionised what your computer can do for you.

This book uses uncomplicated language to help you get the most out of your connection. Each chapter is divided into sections that contain vital information about each topic as well as expert tips and website recommendations to help you along the way. Learn how to protect your computer, keep in touch with instant messaging and PC phone calls, and surf the web without wires both at home and on the move. A Jargon Buster is included at the back of the book to explain any unfamiliar terms.

Chapter One:
Choosing Broadband

Section 1:
Broadband Explained

Essential Information

Going online used to be about connecting your computer to your home telephone and dialling in to surf the web. This is known as dial-up Internet access and although it will get you online, it's slow. There are lots of new and exciting websites and services you can't use with a dial-up connection unless you're prepared to wait and wait and wait.

Broadband allows you to surf the web at high speed. It still uses your telephone line (or cable service), but squeezes a lot more information down it at much faster speeds, opening up new ways to communicate and be entertained.

Section 2:
Benefits of Broadband

Cost

With dial-up Internet you pay as you go. You can also buy Pay As You Go broadband but more usually it involves a monthly fee. It still works out less expensive so if you spend over eight hours a month during peak times on the Internet, you would be better off with broadband.

Talk and Surf
All broadband services allow you to surf the web and chat on your home phone at the same time.

Always On
With dial-up Internet access, switching on your computer and dialling is a hassle. With broadband, your connection is always switched on so you can get online instantly

Communicate
Broadband opens up new and free opportunities to keep in touch with your friends and family.

Music and Video
Broadband is perfect if you love music or films. Millions of music tracks are at your fingertips and broadband makes watching TV and video online a reality.

Online Gaming
Broadband allows you to connect to game players worldwide using your computer or games console. Why play against the computer when you can play against real people?

Wireless Networks
More and more people have several computers in the home. One in the office, one for the kids, even one in

the kitchen. Broadband lets you hook them all together without the need for all those wires.

Security

Keeping your computer safe from hackers and viruses is vitally important. Broadband allows you to download regular updates to your computer so it's always safe from prying eyes.

Section 3:
How to Get Broadband

There are four simple steps you need to take before you sign up to a broadband service.

1. Find out what type of broadband service you can receive.
2. Check out the main broadband providers.
3. Understand what equipment you'll need.
4. Learn what to look for before you buy.

Section 4:
Types of Broadband

Fig. 1 shows that there are three different types of broadband. It's important to decide which is right for you. A lot will depend on which service is available where you live. For most people this is ADSL.

ADSL

What is it?	ADSL stands for Asymmetric Digital Subscriber Line. It means that you can use your existing home telephone to get connected to broadband.
What's the benefit?	In the UK it's widely available to a majority of homes. When you order ADSL you get all the kit and software you need in the post and you install it yourself.
Any disadvantages?	You might be unlucky enough to live in a rural area that doesn't offer ADSL. And if you live a long way from your nearest broadband telephone exchange, you may only be able to get a restricted speed of service. ADSL also uses the same telephone line in your street. If many people in your street have ADSL and are online at the same time, performance can be affected.

CABLE

What is it?	This brings broadband into your home via your TV cable service. The cable company runs a wire from your street straight into the back of your computer.
What's the benefit?	It's just like ADSL but you'll find faster services on cable. Cable can be a great deal if you already have cable TV or bundle it with a cable telephone package.
Any disadvantages?	Cable isn't widely available. In the UK it covers less than 50% of homes. If you don't like the idea of running cables around your house it's not ideal. Like ADSL, you can also suffer speed restrictions if everyone in your street is using it at the same time.

SATELLITE

What is it?	Broadband using a satellite dish attached to your home or garden.
What's the benefit?	Really only for people in isolated areas who cannot get ADSL or cable.
Any disadvantages?	It's more expensive, incurs high set-up charges and only offers slower broadband speeds. Satellite is limited to being up to 10 times faster than dial-up Internet and if you want to upload information to the Internet rather than download, it's slow – only 5 times as fast. Poor weather can also interrupt the connection.

Fig. 1

Section 5:
Which Broadband Service Can You Receive?

Essential Information

To find out which service you can receive, you need to do the following:

Action 1

In the UK go online and visit bt.com/broadband. Enter your BT phone number or postcode (if you don't have a BT phone line) to see if you can get ADSL and what speed of service is available to you (Fig. 2).

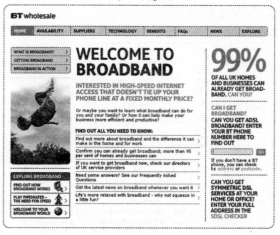

Fig. 2

Action 2

Visit the main cable broadband providers at telewest.co.uk and ntl.com. Enter your postcode to see if you can get their service.

Action 3

If you are unable to receive either ADSL or cable you probably live in a rural or remote location. You should therefore consider a satellite service.

Most people will only have one option but if you have a choice, choose cable – it gives you faster speeds and can be bundled with other phone and digital TV packages.

Section 6:
Finding a Broadband Provider

Visit the websites in Fig. 3 (using a Pay As You Go dial-up account if your computer isn't yet connected to the Internet) to see the latest offers and deals from the most popular UK broadband providers. For details of broadband providers in other countries, visit broadband.thelist.com.

Type of Broadband	Provider
ADSL	AOL : aol.co.uk/broadband BT Yahoo! : btyahoo.com Demon : www.demon.net Madasafish : madasafish.com OneTel : onetel.co.uk Tiscali : tiscali.co.uk/broadband UK Online : ukonline.co.uk Virgin : virgin.net/internetaccess Wanadoo : wanadoo.co.uk

| Cable | NTL : ntl.com
Telewest : blueyonder.co.uk |
| Satellite | AVC : avcbroadband.com
Central Point : www.cpsat.co.uk
skyDSL : teles-skydsl.co.uk |

Fig. 3

Section 7:
What to Look Out For

Essential Information

Buying broadband for the first time or switching to a new service can be a little confusing. There are lots of companies offering different speeds and deals which makes it hard to get straightforward advice. Look out for these four things before you sign up.

Speed

Broadband comes in different speeds, which is measured in megabits per second (or Mb for short). Services of 2 Mb are common but in certain areas or with cable services, you can get 8 Mb or more. But how fast do you really need to go? For occasional use, a speed of 1 Mb or 2 Mb is the most you're likely to need. If you want to download lots of music and photos, or watch online videos, 2 Mb or higher would be preferable. Even faster services don't actually make using the Internet any quicker, they are of most benefit if you will be downloading lots of music and files from the Internet. Fig. 4 shows you how quick each service is.

How long does it take to download a...	Normal dial-up	1Mb Broadband	2Mb Broadband	8Mb Broadband
Standard web page.	15 secs	¾ sec	½ sec	½ sec
1MB digital photo from your e-mail.	3 mins	8 secs	4 secs	1 sec
3MB music track from a website.	9 mins	30 secs	15 secs	4 secs
600MB movie	30 hours	100 mins	50 mins	12 mins

Fig. 4

EXPERT TIP

Megabit (Mb) refers to the speed at which information flows from the Internet down your phone or cable line into your computer. Don't get megabit confused with megabyte (or MB for short). A megabyte refers to the size of a file not the speed. For example a digital photo might be 1 MB in size and a typical music track could be 3 MB. Gigabyte (or GB) is a very large file size and is equivalent to 1,000 MB.

Usage Restrictions

There are three further types of broadband package you can buy: unlimited, restricted or Pay As You Go. Unlimited lets you surf the web and download as much as you want but it costs more per month to buy. Restricted services put a cap on what you download, measured in gigabytes or by the number of hours you're online.

Restricted services offer great value. The caps put on them are enough for most people and if you go over your limit you won't get cut off; you just have to pay a supplement to use more. With a basic 1GB restriction you can enjoy 76 hours a month of Internet surfing, download 240 music singles, listen to 36 hours of web radio or a mixture of all three.

Alternatively, there are a small but growing number of Pay As You Go services. You just pay for how much you use every month. This is cost effective for occasional Internet users.

Free Equipment

To tempt you into buying broadband, many providers offer free equipment when you sign up, such as a modem or free connection. You should check that technical telephone support is free, as many charge premium rates for any help you may need. A thirty-minute call to solve a problem could cost you the equivalent of three or more months' subscription.

Minimum Contracts

Look at the length of the minimum contract – some providers make you stay with them for 12 months, which is fine if you're happy with them but can be problematic if you have any difficulties with their service. Ask if they upgrade existing customers for free when faster and cheaper services become available.

Section 8:
Essential Equipment

When you buy broadband you'll need a number of pieces of equipment in order to get connected.

Computer

You will of course need a desktop computer or laptop. If you've got an old computer it may struggle, so getting broadband can be a good excuse to upgrade. You'll need a PC with at least this specification:

Pentium II or higher
32 MB of RAM memory
CD-ROM drive
At least one USB port
50MB of spare disc space
Windows 98 software or higher

Action 1

Check if your existing computer meets these requirements by going to **Start**, **Control Panel**, **Performance and Maintenance** then **System**.

A Phone or Cable Line

If you opt for a cable service, the line will be fed straight into your home. If you have a cable TV or phone you'll already have the line connected. If you choose ADSL, check that the company that provides your phone service is compatible with broadband. Standard British Telecom phone lines are compatible if broadband is available in your area.

Modem

A modem converts information that is sent or received by your computer from your phone line. You'll need a special high speed modem for broadband. Many providers will give you one for free when you sign up. Most connect to the USB socket on your computer.

Action 2

Check the back of your computer to see if you have at least one USB socket. All modern computers do; it is either a thin oblong socket about half an inch wide or square in a similar shape to the outline of a house. If not you'll need to buy a USB expansion card from your local computer store. Alternatively if you have an Ethernet socket (which looks like a normal telephone socket) you can buy an Ethernet compatible modem.

Microfilters

You'll only need microfilters if you choose ADSL. Microfilters are small connectors that plug in to each of the normal phone sockets in your house (Fig. 5). The filter splits your phone line to allow it to accept both normal telephone calls and broadband Internet. You can only have up to four telephones plus broadband in your home at any one time.

Fig. 5

Section 9:
Switching Broadband Providers

Essential Information

The speed of broadband services continues to rise and the cost continues to fall. So, it can happen that the amazing deal you got six months ago is suddenly not that great any more. But with a little planning you can get as good a deal as new customers do.

Action 1

Don't switch services if you're still in your minimum contract period. This avoids costly cancellation charges.

Action 2

Call your current service provider and tell them you're thinking of leaving them. Most have a team who will do their best to keep you by offering you a new deal or free monthly subscriptions.

Action 3

If you've already got ADSL and decide to switch, ask your current service for your MAC code. This is your 'Migration Authorisation Code'. Give it to your new service provider and they'll then do all the hard work in switching you over. Not all Internet providers use MAC codes, however.

EXPERT TIP

Look for services that don't charge you a fee if you switch to them. Taking on customers from other providers actually costs less than a new customer as you've already got a broadband line and modem installed.

Section 10:
What Type of Surfer Are You?

Here are eight types of web surfer who could benefit from broadband. Find the one that matches your needs the closest, to help decide the best broadband service for you.

Internet Shopper

Likes to buy online and just wants a faster way to surf and shop.

Best choice: 1 Mb restricted service. Avoid services with added value features and exclusive content you're unlikely to use.

Technophobe

Wants a high speed Internet connection without lots of technical jargon and know-how.

Best choice: 1 Mb or 2 Mb restricted service. Go for one with free or low cost technical support.

Music Maestro

Wants to manage and download music tracks to their iPod or MP3 player and listen to live Internet radio.

Best choice: either a 2 Mb unlimited service or one with a monthly restriction of at least 5 GB.

Photofanatic

Likes to take lots of digital photographs and share them with friends online.

Best choice: a restricted service will be fine but go for a fast service of at least 2 Mb so uploading photos to the Internet is much quicker.

Online Gamer

Looking to play the latest games with friends all around the world.

Best choice: the fastest speed unlimited service you can afford, or one with a high monthly usage restriction.

Wireless Wonder

Needs a wire-free Internet connection for their laptop at home.

Best choice: any service is suitable but if you're creating a home network with multiple computers go for at least 2 Mb speed and 10 GB monthly restriction.

Home Worker

Wants a fast Internet connection for their small business or home office.

Best choice: 2 MB restricted service with high monthly allowance. Ensures you can send and receive large e-mail attachments.

Diehard Downloader

Spends large amounts of time online, downloading and sharing lots of video, music and software.

Best choice: the fastest unlimited service you can afford.

Chapter Two:
Getting Started

Section 1:
Installing Broadband

Essential Information

If you've opted for cable broadband, the only thing you have to worry about is being in when the engineer knocks on your door. They'll do all the installation for you. If you've chosen ADSL broadband, you'll receive an installation pack in the mail that includes:

CD-ROM
Broadband modem
Microfilters

Action 1

Put the CD-ROM in your disc drive. It should start automatically. If it doesn't click on **My Computer** from the desktop and choose your CD-ROM drive. Follow the on-screen instructions to install all the software your PC will need to get set up. You may be asked to enter your user name and password which comes with your installation pack. Make a note of these for future use. Restart your computer before continuing.

Action 2

Plug your broadband modem into the Ethernet or USB socket (Fig. 1) on your PC. Your PC will recognise it with a **Found New Hardware** message. Follow the on-screen instructions to install it.

Fig. 1

Action 3

Plug your modem into one of the microfilters using the supplied telephone cable. The sockets on the modem and microfilter will be labelled **ADSL**. Then plug the microfilter into your phone socket.

EXPERT TIP

If your phone socket is far from your computer, buy a longer modem cable rather than using a standard telephone extension lead.

Action 4

Go to the other phone sockets in your house and plug the phone into each of your other microfilters. Then plug the other end of the microfilter into each phone socket – otherwise your home phone won't work. Ensure that all devices that plug into your phone line have a microfilter (such as a fax or satellite TV box).

Action 5

Click on the icon on your desktop for either your Internet browser (such as Internet Explorer) or for your broadband service provider. You'll be connected automatically although in some cases you may be asked to enter your user name and password from your installation pack.

Section 2:
Testing Your Speed

Essential Information

How do you know your broadband service is as quick as you think it is? Whether you've just installed the service or had it for years it's important to check your speed occasionally to ensure you're getting what you're paying for.

Action 1

First of all run a speed test. You can find these online. A good speed test can be found on the ZDNet website at zdnet.co.uk/misc/band-test. Click on **Test my bandwidth**. The website will test your connection and display the results (Fig. 2). The speed is measured as an approximate figure in kilobits per second (or Kbps for short). A megabit or 'Mb' is 1,000 kilobits. If the speed test gives you a result of 2023 Kbps, this is equivalent to 2.023 megabits or approximately 2 Mb. If you've purchased a 2 Mb broadband service, this result would confirm you're getting the correct speed.

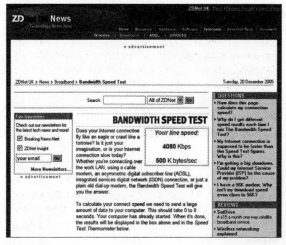

Fig. 2

Action 2

If you're running slower than you expected, run the test again at different times of the day. You may find it runs slower at peak times. You should also check the website of your Internet provider. If there's a problem with their service it will be displayed in their support or help pages, which are easily accessible from their home page.

Other Speed Test Websites:

ADSL Guide
adslguide.org.uk/tools/speedtest.asp

Intel
intel.com/personal/resources/broadband

Test my Speed
testmyspeed.com

DSL Reports
dslreports.com/stest

EXPERT TIP

If your broadband connection goes down due to problems with your service provider make sure you have a backup dial-up Internet service, just in case.

Section 3:
Optimising Your Speed

Essential Information

No matter what speed broadband you have, you can tweak your computer settings to improve your connection. This is really only necessary if you regularly get a slow speed test result or want to squeeze the absolute maximum out of your connection.

Tuning Software

A good tool to use is Dan Elwell's Broadband Speed Test which you can find at broadbandspeedtest.net. The basic version is free to download. Or visit totalidea.com for a copy of Tweak-XP which automatically optimises those computers with Windows XP. Note that some broadband providers frown upon using software to speed up your connection, so they may refuse to help you if you experience problems when tweaking your speed.

Web Accelerators

To improve your Internet browsing you could also consider a web accelerator. This is software that downloads web pages more efficiently by storing frequently used pages on your computer. You can download SpeedOptimizer, which is a good web accelerator, by visiting speedoptimizer. com. Or try Google Web Accelerator which is designed for broadband users. Download it at webaccelerator.google. com. Accelerators make web surfing a bit quicker but won't speed up downloading files such as music or video.

Section 4:
Optimising Downloads

Essential Information

If you'll be using broadband to download lots of music, video or other files then it can be worthwhile using a download manager. They help optimise your download speeds and resume downloads if there is a connection problem. Three download managers you can use are:

GetRight
getright.com

Internet Download Manager
internetdownloadmanager.com

Star Downloader
stardownloader.com

EXPERT TIP

If you're going to be a heavy downloader you'll probably leave your computer on overnight or all day. If your computer is left unattended for some time it may switch itself off, stopping any download. To prevent this from happening change the **Power Options** on your computer.

Action 1
Click on **Start**, **Control Panel**, **Performance and Maintenance** and then select **Power Options**.

Action 2
Change the settings for **Turn off hard disks** as well as **System standby** and **System hibernates** (Fig. 3). Set these to several hours or **Never** to ensure the computer doesn't switch itself off if left unattended.

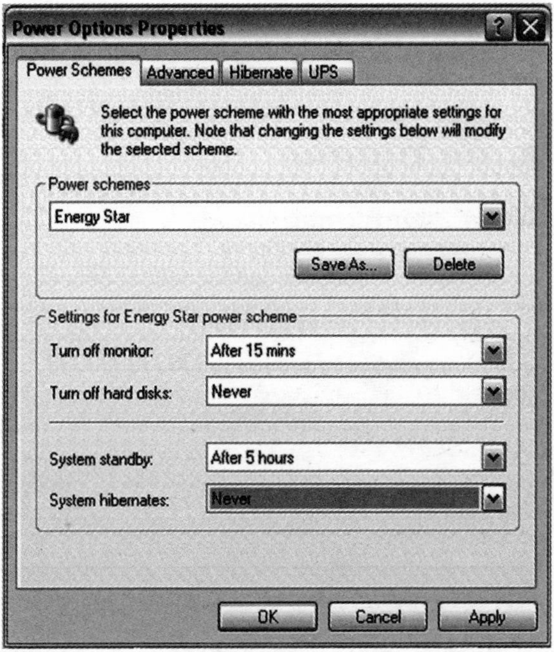
Power Options Properties
Power Schemes
Advanced
Hibernate
UPS
Select the power scheme with the most appropriate settings for this computer. Note that changing the settings below will modify the selected scheme.
Power schemes
Energy Star
Save As...
Delete
Settings for Energy Star power scheme
Turn off monitor:
After 15 mins
Turn off hard disks:
Never
System standby:
After 5 hours
System hibernates:
Never
OK
Cancel
Apply

Fig. 3

Chapter Three:
Protecting Your Computer

Section 1:
Viruses Explained

Essential Information

A computer virus is a lot like a human one. It is an infection that gets into your computer and damages it. Viruses can enter your computer in many ways such as by e-mail or when downloading files from the Internet. They then spread by forwarding themselves to other people online. Some viruses cause minor damage but can be easily removed with the right tools. Others can really mess up your computer.

Hackers

Hackers are individuals, often criminals, who gain access to your computer without your permission. Often they'll gain access using a virus. Most viruses are anonymous, meaning that they infect your computer but cannot personally identify you. But if a hacker's virus infects your computer, it can allow the hacker to spy on what you are doing or access your private files.

What Can Happen to Your Computer?

Here are a few examples of what might happen if your computer is infected by a virus or targeted by a hacker:

- Your computer gets corrupted preventing you from using essential software or accessing the Internet.

- The virus automatically sends itself to everyone in your e-mail address book, infecting your friends as well as you.

- You might accidentally download a hacker's monitoring software that records your Internet and password activity. A hacker can then easily assume your identity or access your online bank.

- Your computer is used to attack other computers or organisations via the Internet without your knowledge.

Section 2:
Viruses and Broadband

Essential Information

Broadband's always-on connection makes you vulnerable to virus and hacker attacks. Hackers use automated programs that scan the Internet for broadband computers with holes in their security. Your high-speed connection means that attacks can happen in the background without any noticeable effect on your computer. You'll be downloading lots of music, games and software in which viruses can easily hide.

Amazingly lots of people don't protect their computers properly. But it's absolutely essential, and with a little bit of preparation, your computer (and all your files, photos and e-mails) can be protected.

Section 3:
Four Steps to Protect Your Computer

There are four simple and inexpensive steps you must take in order to protect your computer from viruses and hackers:

1. Use a firewall.
2. Get anti-virus and spyware protection.
3. Use anti-virus and automatic updates.
4. Backup your computer.

Section 4:
Firewalls

Essential Information

A firewall is just that: a wall of fire that surrounds your computer to protect it. It is software that monitors information flowing to and from your computer and only lets through legitimate traffic. It also helps to 'hide' your computer from hackers. Once installed it runs constantly in the background so you don't have to set it up again.

Choosing a Firewall

Download one of these best-selling firewalls. Although there are some free versions available, you'll have to pay for most other firewalls, but it is money well spent.

Norton Personal Firewall

symantec.com

ZoneAlarm Free Version
zonelabs.com

Windows Firewall
Designed for Windows XP, Windows Firewall comes free with Windows Security Centre, which can be downloaded from the Microsoft website. This is explained in Section 5 of this chapter.

Section 5:
Downloading Windows Security Centre

Essential Information
With Windows XP, one of the best ways to keep your computer protected is Windows Security Centre. This is included as part of Service Pack versions 2 and later. Service Packs are created by Microsoft about once a year with major security updates for your computer. To get a free Service Pack you simply need to download it from the Microsoft website.

Action 1
Log on to update.microsoft.com. This is a clever website that automatically scans your computer and tells you which Service Packs and free software updates from Microsoft it requires. Click on the **Express** button to begin scanning your computer (Fig. 1).

Fig. 1

Action 2

You will be given a list of the updates your computer needs. Select all of them or at least those marked as high priority. This will include the Security Centre if you don't already have it.

Action 3

The updates will then install. The Security Centre is a large file and installing it can take over half an hour, even with broadband. Follow the on-screen instructions to complete the installation.

Once installed, you'll find the Security Centre by clicking on the **Start** button on your desktop and then **Control Panel**. Fig. 2 shows you what it looks like. The Security Centre has three sections: Firewall, Virus Protection and Automatic Updates.

EXPERT TIP

With Windows XP, if you cannot see the Security Centre in Control Panel then you've probably got your system set to **Classic View**. This is the older style of Windows desktop. To change this to the more user friendly **Category View**, click on **Switch to Category View** in the top left of the Control Panel window.

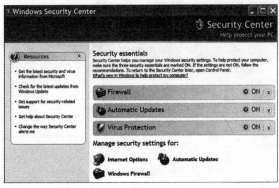

Fig. 2

Section 6: Using the Firewall

Essential Information

If the firewall encounters software on the Internet trying to connect to your computer it will block it and pop-up a message to tell you (Fig. 3). You must then choose to keep blocking it or to unblock it. Check what the program is. To begin with it's likely to be your instant messaging program or your e-mail software. These are fine. But if it's a program you don't recognise, block it.

Action 1

Make sure your firewall is turned on. Open the Security Centre and click on the **Firewall** button on the right to switch it on. The Security Centre will then configure all your settings automatically.

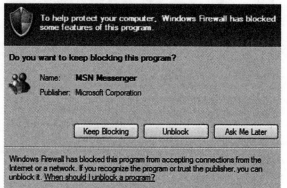

To help protect your computer, Windows Firewall has blocked some features of this program.

Do you want to keep blocking this program?

Name: **MSN Messenger**
Publisher: Microsoft Corporation

[Keep Blocking]   [Unblock]   [Ask Me Later]

Windows Firewall has blocked this program from accepting connections from the Internet or a network. If you recognize the program or trust the publisher, you can unblock it. When should I unblock a program?

Fig. 3

EXPERT TIP

Your firewall should work fine without the need to tweak the settings. If you want to do this however, go to the Security Centre and choose **Manage security settings for Windows Firewall**. Select the **Exceptions** tab to see the list of software to which you've already given permission to access your computer. Untick any of the software in the list if you wish to remove permission.

Section 7:
Virus Protection

Essential Information

Anti-virus protection is your next level of defence in the war against online attacks. A firewall does not scan your computer for viruses or check if you download one when you open an e-mail. Therefore proper virus protection is important to keep out viruses such as Trojan horses and worms.

Choosing Anti-Virus Software

To get virus protection you'll need to download anti-virus software. Good basic packages can be downloaded for free but you'll have to pay for advanced protection.

Free Anti-Virus Software:

AntiVir PersonalEdition Classic
free-av.com

avast! Home Edition
avast.com

AVG Anti-Virus Free Edition
free.grisoft.com

vCatch
vcatch.com

Other Anti-Virus Software:

BullGuard
bullguard.com

Norton AntiVirus
symantec.com

McAfee VirusScan
mcafee.com

Trend Micro PC-cillin
trendmicro.com

Section 8:
Using AVG Anti-Virus

Action 1
One of the best choices for virus protection is AVG Anti-Virus. Download AVG Anti-Virus Free Edition and follow the on-screen instructions to install.

Action 2
Click the **Start** button to find AVG Anti-Virus in your list of **Programs**. The first time you use it, click the **Check for updates** button, which downloads defences against all the latest viruses. You should also run a complete scan of your computer by clicking on the **AVG Test Centre** and selecting **Scan Computer** (Fig. 4). If any viruses are

found, AVG will alert you or you can set AVG to destroy them automatically.

Fig. 4

For more advanced protection you should upgrade to the full version of AVG Anti-Virus for a small fee. As with all anti-virus software, AVG will then work in the background protecting your computer.

Section 9:
What To Do If You've Been Infected

Essential Information

If your computer catches a virus and you don't already have anti-virus protection, there are a number of useful free tools you can find online. Don't use these as a substitute for full anti-virus software. These tools don't run on your computer and don't keep watch 24 hours a day.

Action 1

If you know the name of the virus that has infected your computer, you can find the cure on the Symantec Removal Tools website by visiting securityresponse.symantec.com/

avcenter and choosing **View all Threats** to find your virus from an alphabetical list. If you cannot find the virus listed you can also look for it on the list of Recent Threats on the McAfee website at uk.mcafee.com/virusinfo.

Action 2

If that doesn't solve the problem, use the Microsoft Malicious Software Removal Tool. This checks for bugs and cleans them out and is updated monthly. You can find it at microsoft.com/malwareremove.

Action 3

These tools should catch most major viruses. If you still can't remove the infection, the anti-virus tools on the following websites will help:

Housecall

housecall.trendmicro.com

BitDefender

bitdefender.com

a² free

emsisoft.com/en/software/free

Section 10:
Anti-Virus Updates

Essential Information

Security is a game of cat and mouse. Hackers continually find new holes in software to attack you, whilst software manufacturers create patches or updates to counteract them. If you don't keep up to date with these patches your computer might as well be unprotected. One of the benefits of broadband is that you can download patches quickly and easily.

You must download free virus updates to your computer, either direct from your anti-virus software or from the software manufacturer's website. For example, in AVG Anti-Virus you must periodically click the **Check for updates** button to get the latest protection.

Action 1

In Windows Security Centre (see Section 5 of this chapter) turn on **Virus Protection**. This automatically monitors your anti-virus software and knows if the list of viruses needs to be updated. If it does, a reminder message will pop up next time you turn on your computer (Fig. 5).

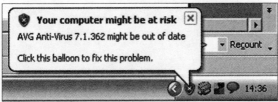

Fig. 5

Section 11:
Spyware

Essential Information

Spyware is software that spies on what you're doing. Most of the time it is advertising related. It watches where you browse then serves up more appropriate advertising when you're online. Some spyware can identify you personally, as well as change your computer settings without your consent. It is normally downloaded by accident or hidden in free software.

Action 1

The best way to remove it is to periodically download and run one of these free anti-spyware tools. They'll hunt down offending spyware and remove them for you.

Spybot Search and Destroy

safer-networking.org

Lavasoft Ad-Aware

www.lavasoftusa.com/software/adaware

Microsoft Windows AntiSpyware

microsoft.com/athome/security/spyware/software

Section 12:
Automatic Updates

Essential Information

Automatic Updates is the third feature in Windows Security Centre. It allows you to download the most recent security patches from Microsoft. You can do this manually by visiting update.microsoft.com but it is better to do it automatically. Broadband enables your computer to download the patches in the background, while you get on with other things.

Action 1

In the Windows Security Centre click on **Manage security settings for Automatic Updates**. Then set a time in the day when you would like your computer to contact the Microsoft website for the latest updates (Fig 6).

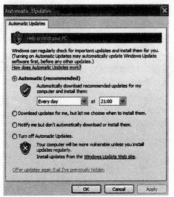

Fig. 6

EXPERT TIP

If you switch your computer off when you're not using it, make sure you choose a time when it is most likely to be switched on.

Section 13:
Backup Your Computer

Essential Information

A backup keeps a copy of important files in case your computer is corrupted by a virus. The simplest way to backup is to save your most important files to a CD-ROM every three to six months and store it in a safe place. Another option is to use online backup.

Online Backup

If your files don't take up lots of space you can save them in a free webmail account such as Hotmail or Yahoo! Mail which offer over a gigabyte of free storage (see Chapter Nine for more on e-mail). Alternatively, you can upload them to an online backup website. These websites allow you to put your files in a safe place from where you can retrieve them should your computer become corrupted.

Iomega iStorage

iomega.com/istorage
Offers up to 5 GB of free storage space for home users. You have to pay a monthly fee to store more.

Xdrive
xdrive.com
You receive up to 5 GB of storage space for a small monthly fee.

Streamload
streamload.com
This website allows you to upload a massive 10 GB of files for free. You can then download up to 100 MB of files per month for free. You have to pay to download more.

Section 14:
Five More Tips to Keep Your Computer Protected

Upgrade Your Computer
If you have an older computer, invest in an upgrade to the latest operating system, such as upgrading from Windows 2000 to Windows XP. The latest operating systems always have better security features. You'll find operating system software at your local computer retailer.

Don't Trust Every Website
Only download files from websites you trust.

Question Every E-mail
Never open an e-mail or instant messaging attachment from someone you don't know or if you don't recognise the attached file.

Look Out for Scams

Be aware of Internet scams (also known as 'phishing') that try and trick you into handing over your personal or financial details. For up-to-date information on scams and software to help you block them, visit microsoft. com/athome/security/email.

Change to a Limited Account

You are probably set up with an 'Administrator' account on your computer. This means that you own the computer so you can change any settings you want. But if a hacker gets access to your system they also become an administrator and can cause maximum damage. If you're just doing normal day-to-day things on your computer such as surfing the web (rather than installing software), then change to a 'Limited' account. A Limited account is more secure as it will not let you install software or change your computer's system settings.

Action 1

To do this, click on the **Start** button, then **Control Panel**, **User Accounts** and **Create a new account**. Create a new user name and select the option for a **Limited** account. When you switch on your PC, login with this new user name to activate the limited settings. You can always login with your original user name if you need to install software that requires an Administrator account.

Section 15:
Further Help

Microsoft's website includes some great video tutorials on how to protect your computer. If you need more help on how to avoid viruses and hackers, visit one of the following websites:

About
antivirus.about.com

Web Aware
bewebaware.ca

Firewall Guide
firewallguide.com

Get Net Wise
getnetwise.org

Microsoft
microsoft.com/athome/security

Chapter Four:
Instant Messaging

Section 1:
Instant Messaging Explained

Essential Information

Instant messaging allows you to see when your friends are online, so you can chat to each other in real time. It's a bit like sending an e-mail and getting an instant response. Instant messaging works on a standard Internet connection but you need broadband to make the most of it. And best of all, it's completely free.

Section 2:
Choosing an Instant Messaging Service

Essential Information

Unfortunately, most services aren't smart enough to talk to each other so to use instant messaging you and all your friends need to download the same instant messaging service. So the first thing to check is if any of your friends already use instant messaging. If they do, then download the same service. If not, then you can take the lead and choose a service. Which one you choose is down to personal preference, but you'll then have to convince your friends to download the same service. Otherwise you'll be talking to yourself.

There are three main instant messaging services to choose from: MSN Messenger, Yahoo! Messenger and AOL Messenger. Here we concentrate on one of the most popular, MSN Messenger, but they all work in a similar way.

Section 3:
Registering with MSN Messenger

Action 1
Visit messenger.msn.com. Click on the **Download** button to start installation.

Action 2
You can download the software straight away if you already have an MSN or Hotmail e-mail account. If you don't have one of these then you'll have to register for a Microsoft .NET Passport account. Passport gives you access to lots of Microsoft services with one login address. It's free and you'll only have to do it once.

Action 3
When asked, click on **Install** to download the software and then follow the on-screen instructions to complete the set up.

Section 4:
Getting Started with MSN Messenger

Action 1

Start MSN Messenger either from the list of **All Programs** after you click the **Start** button, or by clicking on the Messenger icon in the bottom right of your computer screen

Fig. 1

(Fig. 1). You will be asked for your e-mail address and password the first time you start the program.

Action 2

The main areas of the screen are marked on Fig. 2.

Display picture

Add a contact

Online status

Contact address book

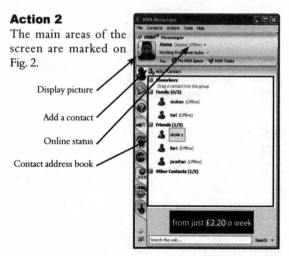

Fig. 2

Action 3

Your **online status** is important as it tells other people when you are online. When you start Messenger, your friends will be notified with a message to say you are there. If you don't want to talk to anyone you can change the status, for example to **Busy** or **On the phone**. Your friends will see that you're there but they won't be able to have a conversation with you. Click on the arrow next to your **online status** to change it (Fig. 3).

Fig. 3

Online

This lets your friends know you're online and willing to talk.

Busy

You can still receive messages when you're busy but Messenger doesn't alert you so you don't get interrupted.

Be Right Back

Shows you're unavailable for a few minutes. You can still receive messages.

Away

Lets your friends know that you can still receive their messages, though they won't get a response. Your online status automatically switches to Away when you're inactive for five minutes

On the Phone

Shows you're busy but you'll be back in a while. You can still receive messages.

Out to Lunch

Tells friends you're not at your computer but will be back later. You can still receive messages.

Appear Offline

Use this when you really don't want to talk to anyone or receive messages – it makes it look like you're not online when you are.

Your friends also have an online status. The icon next to each of your friend's names in your Contact address book (Fig. 4) shows this. Each icon corresponds to those used in Fig. 3. For example, a red icon means your friend is **Offline**, a blue icon means they are **Online**, and a blue icon with

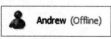

Fig. 4

a 'no entry' sign next to it, means they are **Busy** and
don't want to talk.

Section 5:
Adding a Contact

Essential Information
Your address book is the key to Messenger. You need
to invite friends or 'contacts' to add you to their own
Messenger address books so you can talk to each other.

Action 1
Click on **Contacts**, **Add a Contact** then follow the
simple instructions. Here you can add a contact using your
friend's e-mail address or mobile phone number (Fig. 5).
If they already have Messenger, they will be sent a message
to ask if they want to add you to their address book.

Fig. 5

If they agree you'll get a message back to let you know and their name will automatically appear in your address book. If they disagree it means they don't want to talk to you and your name will be blocked from contacting them in the future. If they don't already use Messenger they'll be sent an e-mail inviting them to download it.

Action 2

Your friends can also send an address-book-invite to you. If they do, you'll get a message asking if you accept their invitation.

EXPERT TIP

You'll notice that each contact in your address book can be organised into one of several folders such as Co-workers, Family or Friends. Moving a name to a different folder is easy. Click on the name once, holding down your left mouse button. Then move your mouse to drag the name across. Release the button to drop the name into the folder.

Section 6:
Sending a Message

Essential Information

Once you have one or more friends in your contact address book you can start using instant messaging.

Action 1

If the icon next to your friend's name is blue/green it means they're online and free to talk. Start the conversation by double clicking on their name or by clicking on **Actions** then **Send an Instant Message**.

Action 2

A new window will pop up – this is called the conversation window. Type your message in the box at the bottom and click **Send**. Your friend will receive this and type you a message in return. As you talk, the transcript of what you've both said appears in the box at the top (Fig. 6).

Fig. 6

Action 3

You can carry on chatting for as long as you want. When you're finished saying goodbye, close the conversation window by selecting **File** from the menu at the top of the window, then choose **Close**.

Receiving a message works in the same way. Your conversation window will pop up with your friend's message and you can reply to them straight away.

EXPERT TIP

If you wish, you can keep a copy of the transcripts of your conversations. Messenger will do this for you automatically. If you wish to switch this off, go to **Tools**, **Options**, and click on **Messages** on the left. Untick the box that says **Automatically keep a history of my conversations**. To review old conversations go to the main Messenger window and choose **File** and **View message history**.

Section 7:
Personalising MSN Messenger

Essential Information

The fun part of messaging is that you can personalise it with pictures, animations and backgrounds.

Action 1

You can add a picture of yourself or anything you want that other people can see when you talk to them (see the Display Picture in Fig. 2). Click on **Tools** and **Change Display Picture**. Select **Browse** to find a picture on your computer (perhaps one taken with your digital camera) and it will automatically appear on the Messenger main screen.

Action 2

You can also change the background image of your conversation window to something more interesting. Click on **Tools**, and then **My Backgrounds** to see a list of available backgrounds. Click on **Browse** to add one of your own from the pictures on your computer– perhaps a picture of your last holiday.

EXPERT TIP

If you have MSN Messenger version 7.5 or later you can also add an animated background. To do this you need to open a conversation window and click on **Backgrounds** then choose one from the list.

Action 3

Tell your friends how you're feeling by adding a personal message next to your name on the Messenger main screen. To add this go to **Tools**, **Options** and then click on **Personal** on the left. Type your message in the box that says **Type a personal message for your contacts to see**.

Action 4

You can even tell your friends what music you're listening to. When you play music in Windows Media Player (see Chapter Six) the song title of what you're listening to will appear on the Messenger main window, instead of your personal message (Fig. 7). To turn on this feature go to **Tools**, **Options**, **Personal** and tick the box that says **Show song information from Windows Media Player**.

Fig. 7

EXPERT TIP

Visit ilovemessenger.msn.com for lots of backgrounds, themes and pictures you can download, or upload your own for others to share.

Section 8:
Emoticons and Winks

Essential Information

When you send a friend a message you can send a lot more than just words. Emoticons and winks are fun cartoon-style animations you can use to express yourself and add more 'personality' to your conversations.

Action 1

Open a conversation window and click on the smiley face which can be found just above the box where you type your message to choose from the available emoticons (Fig. 8) – you could even create your own. While you're 'talking', you can send an emoticon such as a smiley face to show you're happy, or a red face to show you're angry. To create your own, select **Tools**, **My Emoticons** and **Create**. You can choose any picture from your computer and Messenger will turn it in to an emoticon.

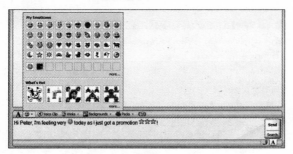

Fig. 8

Action 2

A wink is an animated emoticon with music that fills up the screen and really helps get your point across (Fig. 9). Click on **Winks** (on the same line as the smiley face) and select the one you want to send. You can add more by clicking **Tools** and **My Winks**.

Fig. 9

Section 9:
Sharing Files and Photos

Essential Information
You can also send files, photos and documents to your friends with instant messaging. It's a simple way to share information, especially if the other person lives far away or abroad.

Action 1
To send a file, click on the **Send Files** button at the top of a conversation window. **Browse** to select the file you want to send from your computer. Your friend has to agree to accept the file. Once they do the file will be transmitted (Fig. 10). It might take a while to transfer but you can carry on chatting in the meantime.

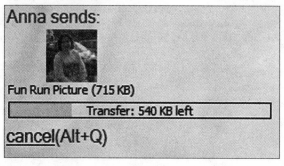

Fig. 10

Section 10:
Voice Messages

Essential Information

You can also talk for free with instant messaging. Both you and the person you're talking to will need a microphone and speakers. Plug them into your computer before you get started.

Action 1

Click on the **Voice** icon located at the top of a conversation window. The first time you use it follow the on-screen instructions which will help set up your microphone and speakers for optimum performance. Your friend will receive a message asking if they want to add voice to your conversation. If they do you can then type and talk at the same time.

Action 2

If you wanted you could send a short voice clip (up to a maximum of 15 seconds) to your friend such as a quick message saying 'Happy Birthday' or inviting them out for dinner. From a conversation window, click and hold the **Voice clip** button (or press and hold F2 on your keyboard). Speak your message, release the button and the voice clip will be sent instantly to your friend. You'll need MSN Messenger version 7.5 or later for this to work.

Section 11:
Webcams and Instant Messaging

Essential Information

A webcam really brings messaging to life as you can see who you're talking to. It's best if both people have a webcam but if you have a webcam and your friend doesn't, that's still fine. They'll be able to see you but you won't be able to see them. Chapter Seven has tips on buying and using a webcam.

Action 1

Messaging with a webcam is very easy. In a conversation window click the **Video** icon at the top of the screen to ask your friend if they want to add a webcam to your conversation. If they accept, the webcam image of your friend will appear automatically on your screen (Fig. 11).

Fig. 11

Action 2

Newer versions of Messenger offer Video Conversation, which make it feel like you're almost there with your friend. This uses your webcam and microphone together so you can see and hear your friend in real time. From a conversation window click on the **Video** icon and choose **Start a Video Conversation**. If your friend accepts, you'll both see and hear each other. Click on the small arrow in the bottom right-hand corner of the webcam image of your friend to see them in full screen on your monitor.

Section 12:
Advanced Features of MSN Messenger

MSN Messenger is invaluable and fun and you'll find there are extra features you can also use.

Whiteboard

Express yourself by doodling with your mouse pointer at the same time as your friend (Fig. 12). You can then copy your artistic creation to another program afterwards. In a conversation window click on **Activities** and then **Whiteboard**.

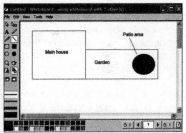

Fig. 12

Remote Assistance

Remote Assistance allows your friend to see your computer screen and take control of it remotely. This is great if they want to show you something on your computer or help you solve a problem. But it is strange watching your friend controlling the mouse pointer on your computer screen. In a conversation window select the **Activities** icon and **Remote Assistance**. Messenger will then invite your friend to switch on Remote Assistance. They'll have to agree before you can start.

Application Sharing

With Remote Assistance you can also share any program on your computer using Application Sharing. You could share Microsoft Word for example and write a letter together or surf the web together to book a holiday or concert tickets. Only one person controls the screen at any one time. Invite your friend to start Application Sharing from a conversation window by clicking on the **Activities** button.

EXPERT TIP

You can send text messages to your friend's mobile phone as well as receive them. If you're not at your computer when your friend replies, Messenger will save their message until the next time you log on. Click the right button on your mouse over any of the contacts in your address book and choose **Add a Mobile Number for this Contact**. If your friend isn't online when you are using Messenger, the icon next to their name will be yellow. This means that you can still send a text message to their mobile phone. To do this, double click on their

---

name in your address book and follow the on-screen instructions. You'll have to buy credits online in order to send a mobile message. It costs about the same as sending a text message from a normal mobile phone. If you don't have credits select **Buy now** after you double click on a contact's name.

Section 13:
Managing Your Privacy

Essential Information

If you switch on your computer to do something specific it can sometimes be distracting to get messages from your friends. So make sure you keep a track of your online status and switch it to **Busy** or something else if you don't want to talk.

Action 1

You must decide whether or not you want Messenger to start automatically when you switch on your computer. To allow Messenger to connect and to launch the program every time you switch on, go to **Tools**, **Options** and click **General**. Tick the box that says **Automatically run Messenger when I log on to Windows** as well as the box that says **Allow automatic sign in when connected to the Internet**.

Action 2

If you want Messenger to connect to the Internet in the background but not to start the program when you start up your computer untick the **Automatically run Messenger**

when I log on to Windows box. That way you can get on with what you're doing and Messenger will only interrupt you if a friend sends you a message.

Action 3

When Messenger starts it will show your status as online and available to talk. But you can choose to start the program with another status such as **Appear Offline**, so you can decide later if you want to let friends know you are there. To do this, start Messenger and before you click to **Sign In** change the status below your password (Fig. 13). Messenger will remember this and will start with the same status in the future.

Fig. 13

Section 14:
Other Messaging Services

AOL Instant Messenger (AIM)
aim.com

AIM allows you to set up multiple identities so you can have different, customised versions of you. That way you can have a more serious one for work and something more relaxed for your friends and family.

Yahoo! Messenger
messenger.yahoo.com
Yahoo! has packed loads of extra features into their messaging service including Stealth Settings which allow you to appear online to some friends and offline to others.

Multiple Messengers
The problem with MSN Messenger, Yahoo! or AIM is that you can only talk to people who use the same service. Multiple messengers are clever enough to talk to everyone no matter which service they use. But they don't have many advanced features such as webcams and mobile messaging. However, they are a good option if all your friends use different instant messaging services, and aren't willing to change to the same one. Two examples include:

Trillian
ceruleanstudios.com

Miranda
miranda-im.org

Section 15:
Web Messaging

Essential Information

All the main instant messaging services have versions you can use on the Internet. This allows you to use instant messaging when you're at another computer (such as at work) or in a web café where you can't download instant messaging software. Login using your usual messaging user name and password – it looks just like the version you have on your home computer.

MSN Messenger
webmessenger.msn.com

Yahoo! Messenger
messenger.yahoo.com/webmsgr

AIM
aimexpress.aol.com

Section 16:
Messaging Security

Essential Information

Unsolicited e-mail is called 'spam' and can contain viruses and offensive or unwanted material. Unfortunately, you can also get unwanted spam instant messages, known as 'spim'. It's not as widespread as e-mail spam but is growing, so do your best to avoid it with these anti-spim and other security tips:

- Avoid giving out personal details when using instant messaging such as credit card details. Be wary of attachments even from friends you know. They might contain a virus.

- If you don't know the person, block them from adding you to their contact address book.

- Avoid meeting someone in person whom you've only met through instant messaging.

- Get the latest security patches for your messaging service. For MSN Messenger use Windows Update (find out more in Chapter Three), or visit messenger.yahoo.com/security if you are using Yahoo! Messenger.

- If you're a parent, you can add controls that restrict when your children can instant message and logs the transcripts of their conversations. MSN Messenger users have to pay for MSN Premium to use this feature. Register for this at join.msn. com. Alternatively, you can buy and download a parental control software package which is compatible with instant messaging services. Two excellent choices are CyberPatrol (cyberpatrol. com) or Netintelligence (netintelligence.com).

Chapter Five:
File Sharing

Section 1:
File Sharing Explained

Essential Information

File sharing is also known as 'peer to peer' file sharing. It allows you to share files such as music, videos and films with anyone else on the Internet. A file sharer uploads or 'posts' their file to the website of a file-sharing network. Anyone else can then visit the website, find the file, and download it to their computer.

File sharing has become hugely popular with millions of broadband users worldwide. A typical music single can be downloaded in seconds and a typical film in a matter of hours. By visiting a file-sharing network you can find millions of files, music and films in an instant.

Section 2:
Is File Sharing Legal?

Essential Information

Using a file-sharing network's website or downloading and using their software isn't illegal. The problem is that downloading some files such as music tracks or films is illegal as the person who shares them doesn't own the copyright. However, people still download copyrighted files because the risk of prosecution for downloading a few music tracks is relatively slim.

You can use file-sharing networks to download files which aren't copyright protected or are free to share. But if you decide to download copyrighted music or films without permission or payment, you are breaching copyright, which is breaking the law, and do so at your own risk.

Due to the popularity of file-sharing copyrighted music and films, there are now a variety of official download websites you can use. The majority offer music with a small number offering films. You have to pay but they are legal and quality is guaranteed. Find out more about downloading music in Chapter Six.

Section 3:
File-sharing Security

Essential Information

Using file-sharing networks can pose a security risk to your computer, as some files aren't what they claim to be and can contain viruses. As long as you have up-to-date anti-virus software, this shouldn't be an issue.

One problem is that most file-sharing networks aren't regulated so you're more likely to find offensive material, especially with films and images. Be wary if you have children who use your PC. Most file-sharing networks have filters to cut out such material, but clever kids can turn them off.

Section 4:
File-sharing Networks

If you wish to try file sharing, there are a number of networks you can choose from:

BearShare
www.bearshare.com

iMesh
www.imesh.com

Kazaa
kazaa.com

LimeWire
limewire.com

The Donkey Network
edonkey.com and emule-project.net

Section 5:
How to Download a File

Action 1
Visit the website of a file-sharing network such as imesh.com.

Action 2

Click on the option to **Download Free iMesh** to your computer. Choose **Run** when prompted and follow the on-screen instructions to complete installation.

Action 3

Start iMesh from your list of **All Programs**. Click on the **Search** button on the left of the screen.

Action 4

Enter a keyword into the **Search** box on the left of the screen. Here you can also choose the type of file you are looking for such as audio or video. Press the **Search** button and a list of available files will appear on the right (Fig. 1).

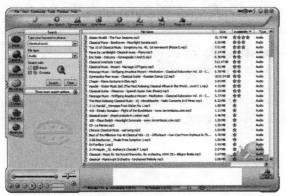

Fig. 1

Action 5

Double click on a file to download it. You can choose several files to download at once. To check the progress of your downloads, click on the **Downloads** button on the left (Fig. 2).

Fig. 2

Action 6

When your download is complete it is stored in the **My Library** area. Click on this button (in the menu bar to the left of the screen) to find the file and double click your mouse over it in order to view or listen to it.

Section 6:
How to Upload a File

If you have a file you wish to share with other people on the iMesh network you can do this by using the iMesh download folder.

Action 1

Right click your mouse over the file you wish to share and select **Copy.**

Action 2

On your desktop, double click on **My Computer** and select your **Local Disc (C:)**. Here you will find a folder named **My Downloads** (Fig. 3).

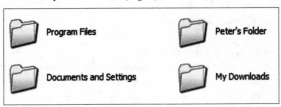

Program Files

Peter's Folder

Documents and Settings

My Downloads

Fig. 3

Action 3

Right click your mouse over the **My Downloads** folder and choose **Paste**. This copies the file you want to share into the folder. Any file you place in this folder can then be searched for by any one of the millions of iMesh users although you have to be running the iMesh program for users to see your shared files. If someone wants your file, iMesh will copy it from your folder directly on to the other user's computer. You can see the progress of the transfer by clicking on the **Uploads** button when using the program.

EXPERT TIP

iMesh is able to share all the files you place in the **My Downloads** folder so make sure you know what you've put in it. It won't share and cannot see the other personal folders and files on your computer. To change which folder iMesh uses as your download folder, go to **Tools**, **Options** and click on **Locations**. Then select **Browse** to choose another folder.

Chapter Six:
Downloading Music

Section 1:
Getting Started

Essential Information

Chapter Five explains file sharing. It's a simple way to download music tracks online but sometimes downloading music on file-sharing networks can be illegal as music is shared without copyright permission.

On legal music download websites you can access thousands of tracks online and download them to your computer or put them on a CD or portable music player. Legal music downloads are not expensive and provide good quality tracks and a wide choice, making music one of the most popular downloads on the Internet.

Before you start you'll need a good media player (see Section 2 of this chapter). You don't have to have a portable music player such as an iPod, as you can simply enjoy downloaded music on your computer. If you have a CD or DVD writer, you can burn music to disc instead.

Section 2:
Media Players

Essential Information

A media player is software that allows you to listen to music as well as watch videos online. The three main media players to choose from are Windows Media Player, RealPlayer and QuickTime, all of which are free.

Action 1

Windows Media Player comes with all new PCs but make sure you download the latest version at microsoft.com/windowsmedia. The latest versions are faster and have more features.

Action 2

Windows Media Player plays most major audio and video files but it doesn't play those recorded in 'Real' format. You should therefore also install RealPlayer (realplayer.com). The free version is good enough for most use although you will be encouraged to pay for the premium version when you download it.

Action 3

These two players will be sufficient for most people, although if you have an iPod you will also need to download the QuickTime media player (apple.com/quicktime).

Action 4

When you select to download each media player, choose **Run** when prompted and the software will download and then start the installation automatically. Follow the on-screen instructions to complete installation.

You don't have to open a media player in order to use it. When you select a music track to listen to, your media player will start automatically for you.

Section 3:
Five Steps to Downloading Music

There are five steps to downloading music online:

1. Choose the right music download software.
2. Decide what type of downloads you want.
3. Choose an online music store and register.
4. Pay, download, listen and enjoy.
5. Put your music on a CD or portable music player.

Section 4:
Music Download Software

Essential Information

If you want to download music from the major online music stores you will need to install software on your computer – don't worry, in most cases it's free. The software connects to the store's website so you can easily find songs. If you have a portable music player you first need to make a decision.

If You Have an iPod

If you have an iPod, the best option is to use iTunes for music downloads. You can download music from other websites but you must import it into the iTunes software to listen to it on your iPod.

If You Have Any Other Portable Music Player

If you have any portable music player other than an iPod (such as Creative Zen or Sony MP3 players) then you cannot use the iTunes store, but you can use any other music download store.

If You Don't Have a Portable Music Player

If you don't have a portable music player and just want to download music to your PC then you can use iTunes or any of the other music download stores. Some stores don't require you to use their software so you can download tracks directly from their website and you can listen to them using Windows Media Player or RealPlayer.

Section 5:
File Formats

Essential Information

File formats describe the way music tracks are compressed into a digital format. The most common is MP3 (portable music players are commonly known as MP3 players). Online music stores offer downloads in either MP3 or WMA format, both of which you can easily play on your computer media player or transfer to an MP3 player. If you have an iPod and use iTunes you'll also be able to use special Apple audio formats.

MP3

The most common type of music file, it can be played on all computers and portable music players. It can store a typical album in a tenth of the space used by a CD. File names always end with '.mp3', such as 'guitarsolo.mp3'.

WMA

Microsoft Windows Media Audio (WMA) is a competitor to MP3. File names end with '.wma'. You can't play music in WMA format in iTunes or on an iPod.

WAV

WAV files are used for recording sound or voice clips on your computer.

AAC and Apple Lossless

Exclusive to iTunes, Advanced Audio Coding (AAC) and Apple Lossless Encoder offer superior sound quality and take up less disk space than MP3 files. File names end with '.m4a' or '.m4p' for AAC and '.ale' for Apple Lossless Encoder.

Digital Rights Management

Also known as DRM, music downloaded from the major music stores includes DRM software. This controls how you can use each music track. For example DRM can let you play a track on your computer but not allow you to copy it. Or it can prevent you playing it on more than one computer. This prevents piracy but also means that with some stores, you have to pay more for a track if you want to do more with it.

EXPERT TIP

Find out which are the most popular MP3 downloads by visiting mp3charts.com or bbc.co.uk/radio1/chart.

Section 6:
Types of Music Download

There are four different types of music download you can enjoy:

Pay Per Track
This allows you to download and own a music track forever. You can then do what you want with it such as burn it to a CD or copy it to an MP3 player.

Unlimited Downloads
You can download as many tracks as you want for a standard monthly fee. Some services, such as Napster, also offer pay per track but if you stop your monthly payments you won't be able to listen to certain pay per track songs you have already purchased.

Streaming

With this you can listen to tracks live through the music store's website or software but you can't record or keep it. Streaming tracks are either included in a monthly subscription or you pay a small fee to listen to each one.

Free

For the widest choice and the latest music you'll have to pay. But you can find free and legal music downloads online. Music stores offer either free preview clips or free promotional tracks (especially for unsigned or up-and-coming bands) on major web portals.

EXPERT TIP

Music retailer Amazon previews albums with free short clips of each song. This can help you decide what songs to download online. Visit amazon.co.uk, or amazon.com for a wider choice of previews.

Section 7:
Using Napster

Essential Information

Napster offers over one million songs and uses the WMA format, so it is compatible with Windows Media Player and all MP3 players.

Action 1

Visit napster.co.uk or (napster.com in the US) to download the Napster software. Click on **Download Napster.** The

File Download pop-up will appear. Select **Run** and follow the on-screen instructions. Tick the **Start Napster Now** box and select **Finish** to complete installation.

Action 2

When you're prompted to register you will have to choose whether to sign up for unlimited downloads for a monthly fee (you'll usually be given a free trial) or if you want to pay per track. To choose to pay per track, select **Start Napster Light**.

Action 3

Now you can sign in (Fig. 1). Tick on **Sign Me In Automatically** if you're the only person to use your computer.

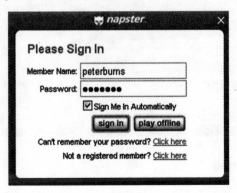

Fig. 1

Action 4

Fig. 2 shows you what the Napster screen looks like. Try out some of the options to get to know it better:

1) Search (by artist or album).
2) Browse Music (categories such as rock or reggae).
3) Library (where all your downloaded music tracks are kept).
4) Features (including NapsterLive – special recordings just for Napster users).
5) Now Playing (details of the current track you are listening to).

Fig. 2

Action 5

Enter a keyword in the search box (for example 'Queen') and click on **Search**. You'll be presented with a list of possible artists (Fig. 3). In this case choose 'Queen' by pressing the arrow icon to the left of the name.

Fig. 3

Action 6

Napster will present you with a list of all the albums and individual tracks you can buy (Fig. 4). To hear a thirty-second preview click the green **30** button. This will automatically play the preview. Simply click on **buy track** and enter your credit card details to complete the purchase. Napster will then automatically download the track to your computer. You can also buy entire albums by selecting the **buy album** button.

Fig. 4

Action 7

If you wish to upgrade to unlimited downloads for a
monthly fee you can do this by going to **My Account** and
then **Account Status**.

Section 8:
Music Download Stores

Pay Per Track Only:

Audible (audio books)
audible.com

Big Noise Music
bignoisemusic.com

MP3.com
mp3.com

MSN Music
music.msn.co.uk (or music.msn.com in the US)

My Coke Music
www.mycokemusic.com

Sony Connect
sonyconnect.com

Pay Per Track and Unlimited Downloads:

Apple iTunes
apple.com/itunes

eClassical
eclassical.com

eMusic
emusic.com

HMV Digital
www.hmv.co.uk

Napster
napster.co.uk (or napster.com in the US)

Virgin Digital
virgindigital.com

Wippit
wippit.com

Free Music:

Download.com
music.download.com

Epitonic
epitonic.com

Garage Band
garageband.com

Karadar Classical Music
www.karadar.com

MP3.com Listening Room
mp3.com/listening_room

Peoplesound
www.peoplesound.com

Sound Click
soundclick.com

Vitaminic
vitaminic.com

Yahoo! Music
uk.launch.yahoo.com (or launch.yahoo.com in the US)

EXPERT TIP

If you like a particular artist or band you'll often find free music tracks or previews on their official website. It's also a good idea to try the website of music record labels such as sonybmgmusic.co.uk.

Section 9:
Transferring Music Downloads to an MP3 Player or CD

Essential Information

Once you've built up a music collection online you may want to burn it to a CD or put it on your MP3 player. If you use a subscription service such as Napster you have to pay more each month if you want to do this. The free software that you get with Napster, iTunes or other music stores helps you transfer music, although you can use the features in Windows Media Player.

Action 1

To transfer music using Napster click on the **Library** button on the top right of the screen (Fig. 2) to see all the songs you have downloaded.

Action 2

Highlight the songs you want to burn by clicking on the name with your left mouse button (hold down the CTRL key to choose multiple tracks) and then right click your mouse and select **Burn Track(s)** (Fig. 5). If you want to save the songs to your MP3 player click on **Transfer Track(s) to Portable Device** instead.

Play
Add to Now Playing
Add to ▶
Download Track(s)...
Delete Track(s)
Burn Track(s)
Transfer Track(s) to Portable Device
Buy Track(s)...
Buy Album...
View Artist Page
View Album Page
Find in Members' Collections
Send Track(s)...
Build Radio Station
Edit Track Data...

Fig. 5

Action 3

Your tracks will appear in the burn window at the bottom of your screen (Fig. 6). To change the playing order click on a track and hold down your left mouse button to drag them to a different position. Release the button to drop it where you want it. Click **Burn** to save them to a blank CD disc in your CD drive.

Fig. 6

Burning to a CD or copying to an MP3 player is slightly different in Windows Media Player.

Action 1
Open Windows Media Player and click on the **Library** tab to see all your music.

Action 2
Create a **Playlist** by clicking on the music tracks you want and, whilst holding down your left mouse button, dragging them over to the right of the screen (Fig. 7).

Fig. 7

EXPERT TIP

You can change the order in which the songs play by dragging them up and down the list to a different position.

The Beginner's Guide to Broadband and Wireless Internet

Action 3

When you are ready, select the **Start Burn** button to burn
the playlist to a CD or select **Start Sync** to add the tracks
to your MP3 player (Fig. 8).

Fig. 8

Section 10:
Listening to Radio

Essential Information

Broadband lets you listen to digital quality radio without
the pauses and problems you'll find with a slower Internet
connection. There are thousands of stations to choose
from so you're guaranteed to find a radio station that's
right for you.

Log on to these popular radio website directories to find
a great station. Once you find a station you want, click on
the name to be taken to its website where you can then
click on the link to listen. This will launch your media
player and start the broadcast.

I Choose Radio

ichooseradio.com

Live 365

live365.com

Radio Directory
radiodirectory.com

Real Radio
radio.real.com

Radio-locator
radio-locator.com

MSN Radio
radio.msn.com

Radio Tower
radiotower.com

TVRadioWorld
tvradioworld.com

vTuner
vtuner.com

Microsoft
windowsmedia.com/radiotuner

EXPERT TIP

It's better to look for stations that broadcast at faster speeds; at least 128k is advisable, although slower speed broadcasts will still sound good.

Section 11:
Using Windows Media Radio Tuner

Essential Information

One of the easiest radio directories to use is the Windows Media Radio Tuner. You'll need the Windows Media Player to use this (see Section 2 of this chapter).

Action 1

Launch Windows Media Player either from the icon on your desktop or by selecting it by clicking on **Start** and then **All Programs**.

Action 2

Using the tabs at the top click on **Guide** then **Radio Tuner**. You'll be given a list of the featured radio stations available to you.

Action 3

If you don't see any you like you can find another by choosing a category in the **Find more stations** section on the right. This will bring up a list of all the stations in that category (Fig. 9). The middle column refers to the speed at which the station transmits (higher speeds make for a clearer sound). Pick one to view details of its playlist. Then either click to visit the website or select **Play** to start the radio broadcast.

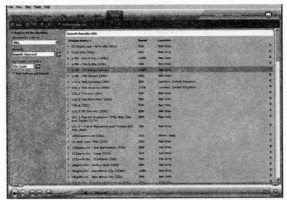

Fig. 9

Section 12:
Podcasts

Essential Information

Listening to live radio is great but unlike normal radio, broadband allows you to listen to a show that you've missed. More and more radio stations allow you to listen to shows that have already been aired by offering them as an MP3 music track you can download from their website.

Radio stations call their MP3 music tracks 'podcasts'. Podcast comes from the phrase 'iPod broadcast'. You don't have to have an iPod, as your computer or any other MP3 player can play podcasts.

Podcasting is different to downloading just one show from a station's website because a podcast knows the next time the show will be aired. Using your broadband connection it then automatically downloads it for you so you've always got the latest edition of your favourite show.

Action 1
To use podcasts you'll first need to download free podcast software. Visit any of the following websites and follow the on-screen instructions to complete installation of the software.

Apple iTunes
apple.com/itunes/download

Juice
juicereceiver.sourceforge.net

jPodder
jpodder.com

Ziepod
ziepod.com

Action 2
Visit a radio station that offers podcasts such as Virgin Radio. Log on to virginradio.co.uk/podcasts and select the show you want to hear.

Action 3
Click on the link to download the latest show (Fig. 10). Save it to a folder (just as you would when downloading any other type of file) and then double click on it to listen.

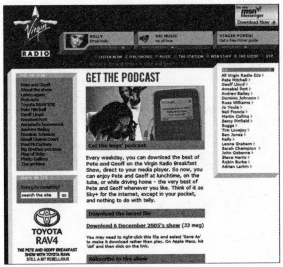

Fig. 10

Action 4

However, you won't get updates for each new show unless you download it as a podcast. To do this copy the website address given for the podcast by highlighting it, right clicking your mouse and choosing **Copy**.

Action 5

Next create a new radio show in your podcast software. For example, if you've downloaded Ziepod software, click on the green '+' icon to **Add Podcast** and then right click your mouse and select **Paste** to place the web address in the **Podcast Feed Address** box (Fig. 11). Click **Finish** to complete the process.

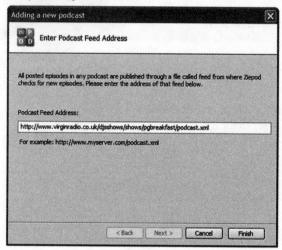

Fig. 11

Podcast Directories
If you don't know whether a radio station offers podcasts, visit one of these directories. You can search a topic such as comedy to receive details of all stations that offer comedy radio show podcasts.

Apple
apple.com/itunes/podcasts

Podcast
podcast.net

Podcast Alley
podcastalley.com

Podcast Bunker
podcastbunker.com

Podcasting News
podcastingnews.com

PodFeeder
podfeeder.com

PODspider
podspider.com

Yahoo!
podcasts.yahoo.com

Chapter Seven:
TV, Video and Webcams

Section 1:
Getting Started

Essential Information

With broadband you can easily watch TV, video clips and even entire films online. In order to view these you'll need a good media player that allows you to listen to music and watch videos: Windows Media Player, RealPlayer and QuickTime are free and easy to use. See Chapter Six for more on these as well as instructions on how to download each media player.

Section 2:
TV and Video on the Web

Essential Information

There are lots of video clips and films you can view on the web and some broadcasters will allow you to watch full television programmes online. However, you're more likely to find shorter video clips than full programmes until more TV companies broadcast more of their programmes on the Internet.

TV Channels

Visit ww.itv.com or webtvlist.com for a directory of live
and recorded TV channels from across the world. Here
you'll find everything from Reuters news (tv.reuters.com)
to the latest space updates from NASA TV (www.nasa.
gov/multimedia). Click on the channel name to watch it
on your media player.

EXPERT TIP

For an easy way to watch TV channels and video clips
online, download Free Internet TV from holersoft.net. It
integrates the various TV websites into one easy-to-use
video player. You can try it for free but you will have to
pay a small charge if you want the full version.

BBC Broadband

An excellent place to start getting news, sport and
entertainment TV online is BBC Broadband.

Action 1

First visit bbc.co.uk/broadband. Here you'll find a list of
all the latest broadband video clips available.

Action 2

Choose a clip. You'll be taken to the relevant part of the
BBC's website. Click on the link to start watching the
video of your choice.

Action 3

When you click on a video link on a website you can
watch it in one of two ways: the website downloads the

clip to your media player which starts the video for you; or the video plays on the website itself (this is known as 'streaming'). The BBC uses the latter and shows videos online in the BBC Player. They have a number of players including music, sports and news (Fig. 1).

Fig. 1

Blinkx TV

Blinkx TV is a website that aggregates video from major TV companies such as Reuters, Fox and CNN. It's a great place to find high quality video clips online.

Action 1

Log on to blinkx.tv. From the home page, you can search on any subject by entering one or more keywords in the search box.

Action 2

Blinkx will then list all the videos you can watch on that topic from a variety of sources (Fig. 2).

Fig. 2

Action 3

Click on the video you want to watch and it will either play in the video box on the right of the window, or you will be taken directly to the website with the video clip, which will start automatically.

Action 4

You can also set up your own video channels with Blinkx. Click on the **Personal TV Channels** link at the top of the page and search for a topic, such as 'motorsports'. Press the **Submit** button to save this as a personal channel. You can then access this channel again next time you visit the website, so it's easier to find videos on your favourite topics.

EXPERT TIP

After your initial search, you can refine your results further using the bar under the search box. Move the bar towards **Date** and your search results will show the latest video clips by date. Move the bar towards **Relevancy** and your search results will more closely target your topic no matter what date they were made.

Other Online TV Channels

You'll find lots of other websites which broadcast their own TV 'channels' online. Many are an amalgamation of shorter video clips. However, TV broadcasters are now looking to offer full programmes online. UK broadcaster Channel 4, for example, airs some shows online before they reach your TV screens. Look out for the BBC's Integrated Media Player, which allows you to watch BBC programmes you may have missed from the past seven days.

3BTV
www.3btv.com

AOL Television
television.aol.com

Apple iTunes
apple.com/itunes/videos

BBC Integrated Media Player
bbc.co.uk/imp

Blueyonder TV
blueyonder.co.uk/tv

Channel 4
channel4.com

GreenGrass
greengrass.tv

ITV Local
itvlocal.tv

Mania TV
maniatv.com

Open Media Network
omn.org

ROO TV
rootv.com

RealGuide
guide.real.com

Smart Streams
smartstreams.com

Tiscali TV
tiscali.co.uk/broadband/tv

TV.com
tv.com

Section 3:
Films on the Web

There's a small but growing number of websites from where you can legally buy and download full films. Try one of these websites or you'll also find plenty of websites with film trailers and short video clips in Chapter Twelve.

Bollywood TV
bollywood.tv

Cinema Now
cinemanow.com

MovieFlix
movieflix.com

Movielink (US only)
movielink.com

Sky By Broadband
www.sky.com/skybybroadband

Section 4:
Searching for Video Clips

Essential Information
You can also search for any type of video clip on the Internet. You may already be familiar with standard search engines such as Google (google.co.uk) or Yahoo! (yahoo.

co.uk). These allow you to find websites by entering keywords on a specific topic. With broadband you can now also use free video search engines that work in exactly the same way. Some video search engines such as Google Video have their own collection of videos you can search. Others such as Singingfish trawl the Internet for videos already online and then link you to the website where you can find them.

Action 1
Try searching for video using Singingfish. Log on to singingfish.com.

Action 2
At the top of the page enter keywords for a topic that interests you. You can also select the type of file you are looking for such as news or audio and other criteria such as the video length. Then click on the **Fish it** button.

Action 3
You'll see a list of all the videos Singingfish could find including the title of the video, further details and length. Click on the title to watch the video (Fig. 3).

Fig. 3

Section 5:
Other Video Search Engines

You can also try these video search engines for more clips
and videos:

AltaVista Video
altavista.com/video

AOL Video
aol.com/video

Excite Video
excite.com

Google Video
video.google.com

Ifilm
ifilm.com

MSN Video
video.msn.com

Truveo
truveo.com

Yahoo! Video
video.search.yahoo.com

Section 6:
Online Video Recorders

Essential Information

If you're using a video search engine (see Section 4 of this chapter) and want to record a video you must save the selected video to your computer when you download it: then you can watch it whenever you want.

However, many websites 'stream' video, such as news, live events or music concerts. You can't save these or radio shows in the same way. To save these shows you need an online video and radio recorder.

Action 1

For a free online video recorder use Bulent's Screen Recorder. Go to thesilver.net and click on **Download**. Follow the on-screen instructions to install it.

Action 2

To do a simple recording, open up the website that has the video you want to record. Go to **Start** and **All Programs** to find and start the Screen Recorder (see Fig. 4).

Action 3

Press **Select Source** and then choose **A Region**. This gives you a box that floats above the webpage from which you wish to record. You can move the box around your screen or resize it using the arrows in the bottom right corner of the box. Fit the box around the section of the webpage that will display the video you wish to record, then press the **Enter** key to confirm.

Fig. 4

Action 4

Select the Screen Recorder window at the bottom of your desktop screen so it reappears. You'll see a row of four buttons at the top. Click on the image of a camera to start recording. Click the **Stop** button to end recording.

Action 5

Click on **Save** to save the video clip to a folder on your computer. You can then open it whenever you want and watch it again.

Action 6

Use the **Configuration** button to change the settings. Here you can tick whether or not you want to record sound with your video clip, display the date or include the mouse cursor in the recording.

EXPERT TIP

You can use the Screen Recorder for many things. If you use a webcam with instant messaging (see Chapter Four) you can record your video conversations or you can use it to record yourself using software on your computer, for demonstrations or presentations.

You'll need to be sure you're not breaking copyright laws by recording website video clips. In some countries recording for your own personal use may be allowed as long as you don't distribute the recording.

Section 7:
Choosing a Webcam

Essential Information

A webcam is a mini video camera you connect to your computer that records pictures and transmits them over the Internet. Even if you have one already you're probably not using it to its full potential.

You're not going to get television quality pictures with a webcam as they are low resolution compared to your TV. But using a good webcam together with broadband will produce higher quality pictures and smoother video clips.

What to Look For

USB Connection

Most webcams connect directly to the USB socket on your computer. If you have an old computer without a USB socket you'll need a camera that plugs into one of your printer sockets.

Resolution

Higher resolution produces a better quality picture. You'll need a webcam with a resolution of at least 320 by 240 pixels and an auto focus lens that adjusts to different lighting. In a dark room webcams don't work so well, so you may also need to buy a desk lamp to light up your face.

Frames Per Second

This is how many shots the webcam takes each second. You will need at least 30 frames per second to obtain smoother video.

Microphone

You'll need one of these to make phone calls online or when using instant messaging, so choose a webcam with a built-in microphone. If your computer is in a noisy room, a separate microphone will be better or you may find yourself shouting at your webcam.

Positioning

Choose a webcam that you can attach easily to the top of your screen or to a stand and that can be tilted both horizontally and vertically.

EXPERT TIP

Logitech's QuickCam range (logitech.com) is a good option. The more expensive models include smart features such as camera zoom and face tracking which automatically moves the camera when you move. Creative (creative.com) or Trust (trust.com) are also worth trying. On the other hand you could choose a digital camera with a built-in webcam such as the Fujifilm Finepix (fujifilm.com).

Section 8:
Connecting a Webcam

Action 1

Connecting your webcam is simple. Your computer will automatically detect the new webcam when you plug it into the USB socket. It will then install the correct software and prompt you through the set up process. Many webcams also come with automatic installation for popular instant messaging programs like MSN Messenger and Yahoo! Messenger.

Section 9:
Video E-mail

Next time you want to send an e-mail to somebody, make it more interesting. Send them a video e-mail instead using your webcam.

Action 1
The software you receive with your webcam will differ from model to model. The software will allow you to record clips just like a video camera and save the video clip file to your computer.

Action 2
You'll need to keep your recording short – a few minutes is probably the most you'll be able to record. This ensures the file size isn't too big to send by e-mail. You can reduce the file size and give yourself more time to speak by altering your webcam software's settings. You can select a lower camera lens resolution, or lower frames per second (go for 15 instead of 30). The video won't be as smooth but it will still be good enough. You can reduce the sound quality, from 16 bit CD quality stereo to simple 8 bit mono. It's still good enough for chatting to your mates.

Action 3
Once you've recorded your video clip, all you have to do is to send it as a normal e-mail attachment to your friends. When they receive your e-mail and open the attachment,

they will be able to see your video message (provided they have an appropriate media player, of course).

Action 4
Instead of using your webcam software to record your video message, you can use the webcam service from Tiscali. Visit webcam.tiscali.co.uk. You don't need to download software or be a Tiscali customer to use this service. Click on **Register Here** to get started.

Action 5
Once you've registered return to the above website and login using your account details. Choose **Video E-mail**.

Action 6
You'll see a page with the live image of your webcam (Fig. 5). Complete the boxes to tell Tiscali your friends' e-mail addresses, and if you wish, you can also type in a message.

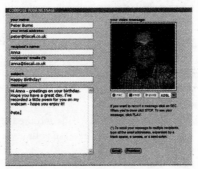

Fig. 5

Action 7

Record a video greeting by pressing **Rec** to start the recording and **Stop** to finish. Then press **Send** and your friends will receive an e-mail invitation to view your video greeting.

Section 10:
Long Video E-mails

Essential Information

If you want to send a longer video that is too large to send by e-mail you can upload the video to a free video e-mail website and then send your friends the link where they can watch it. Alternatively, try one of the ideas for sending large e-mails in Chapter Nine.

Action 1

Record a video as in Section 9 of this chapter. It might be a birthday greeting or a message to your family.

Action 2

Log on to clipshack.com and select **Sign up for a Free Account**.

Action 3

Login with your new account details and use the options on the left to select **Upload**. **Browse** your computer for the video clip you've just recorded with your webcam and ClipShack will upload it to the Internet, into a personal folder. This may take some time.

Action 4

Add a description of the video and decide who can see it. Choose **All my Friends**. You'll then be taken to the **My Clips** area where all the videos you've uploaded are displayed (Fig. 6).

Fig. 6

Action 5

Click on the video you want to send, then choose the **E-mail** option. Enter the e-mail addresses of your friends or family and ClipShack will send them all an e-mail with a website link they can visit, where they can view your video message.

Other Video E-mail Websites:

DropShots

dropshots.com

Mefeedia

mefeedia.com

Mydeo
mydeo.com

Our Media
ourmedia.org

Vimeo
vimeo.com

You Tube
youtube.com

Section 11:
Vlogging

Essential Information

First there was blogging. This is short for 'web logging' and involves creating a personal website (or 'blog') on a favourite subject. People use blogs to record their daily lives, for holiday trips or to tell the world about their favourite hobby. It's a great way to put your life online and to communicate it with friends.

Now there's video blogging or 'vlogging'. It's the same as blogging but using video clips. Try setting up a vlog for yourself.

Action 1

First of all decide what your theme is going to be – you could create a family website or one about your favourite sport. Write some text about it and record one or more video clips using your webcam. For ideas check out vlogs that other people have created at vlogmap.org or vlogdir.com.

EXPERT TIP

For a more professional look you can edit the video clip you've recorded as well as add music or effects using video editing software. Windows Movie Maker (download it at microsoft.com/moviemaker) is an easy-to-learn free package.

Action 2

Register with a free blogging website. This will create the webpage that your friends can visit to see your videos. Try the popular blogger.com and register for a free account. Blogger.com lets you create your own personal webpage but it won't store your video clips for you. You'll need to load your videos to a free video storage website (there's a list of these in Section 10 of this chapter) and create a link from your Blogger personal webpage to your video clips.

Creating a vlog does require a little technical know-how. If you get stuck you'll find help at videoblogging.info, groups. yahoo.com/group/videoblogging, or watch the handy video guide to getting started at freevlog.org.

Section 12:
World Wide Webcams

Webcams are popular all over the world and thousands of people have put their own webcam footage on the Internet for you to see. Some are of people's homes, others are of famous landmarks. If you like the idea of seeing what's happening elsewhere in the world right now, visit one of these webcam directories for a list of thousands of webcams you can watch.

WebCam Central
camcentral.com

Camvista
camvista.com

EarthCam
earthcam.com

Webcam Search
webcamsearch.com

Chapter Eight:
PC Phone Calls

Section 1:
PC Phone Calls Explained

Essential Information

You can use your broadband connection to make phone calls over the web. Internet phone calls are much cheaper than standard home or mobile phone calls and can also be free. They're an especially good option for calling friends or family abroad.

There are two ways you can talk over the web. One option is to use instant messaging. This allows you to talk, type, and even see who you're talking to with a webcam. Find out all about instant messaging in Chapter Four. Alternatively, you can use a Voice-over-Internet service. This is also known as 'voice-over-IP' (the IP stands for Internet Protocol). What it means is that instead of sending e-mails or pictures to your friends when you're online, you 'send' them your voice.

All the major Voice-over-Internet services are secure, so you can be sure no one is listening in on your conversations. In addition, the sound quality is better than a standard telephone because it's digital.

Section 2:
Headsets and Handsets

Essential Information

To make phone calls on your PC you'll need a microphone to talk into and speakers to hear with. You probably already have speakers with your computer (or built into your monitor) so you can either buy a separate microphone or better still buy an all-in-one headset.

Headsets

Just like the ones used in call centres, all-in-one headsets leave your hands free to type. They cost about the same price as a standard telephone. Logitech do a good range of stereo headsets (logitech.com) and Plantronics sell headsets already bundled with Skype Voice-over-Internet software (plantronics.com). Plug the headset into the USB socket at the back of your PC.

Handsets

There are a growing number of Internet-enabled telephones that plug straight into your computer, again using the USB socket. They're aimed at people who want to save money using Voice-over-Internet but don't like using a headset. You'll receive easy-to-follow set-up software when you buy a handset.

Section 3:
Choosing a Voice-over-Internet Service

Essential Information

There are a number of Voice-over-Internet providers you can choose from. You'll find there are two types: pay monthly or Pay As You Go. Phone companies that offer all-inclusive monthly talk packages, such as Vonage (vonage. co.uk), give you a telephone handset that plugs into your computer and lets you call other Vonage customers for free or other people at selected rates.

However, if you don't want to pay a monthly fee choose an Internet-based Pay As You Go service. There's BT Communicator (bt.com/btcommunicator), Google Talk (google.com/talk) or Skype (skype.com).

These allow you to talk for free to friends who use the same service. However, if you want to talk to people who don't have a PC or who have a normal telephone, BT Communicator and Skype allow you to do this at competitive call rates. Here we look at how to use Skype, one of the first Internet phone services. Don't worry, you'll find they all work in the same way.

Section 4:
Getting Started with Skype

Action 1

Download Skype by visiting their website. There's even a special version that Mac users can download. Follow the on-screen instructions to install the program. You'll have to choose a Skype user name (which doesn't have to be your real name; a nickname will do) and a password.

Action 2

Once it's installed, you can start Skype from the **All Programs** menu on your desktop and get to know the Skype main window (Fig. 1).

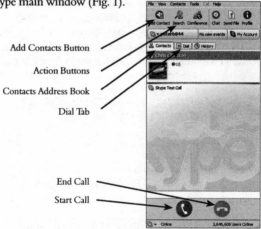

Add Contacts Button

Action Buttons

Contacts Address Book

Dial Tab

End Call

Start Call

Fig. 1

Section 5:
Adding Contacts

Essential Information
The contacts address book is like your normal telephone address book. You need to add contact details for your friends and family before you can call them.

Action 1
To do this, click on the **Add Contact** button or click on **Contacts**, then **Add a Contact**.

Action 2
Enter the Skype name if you know your friend already uses Skype. If you don't know their Skype name, contact them to ask them what it is. Alternatively, you can find them in the Skype worldwide telephone directory. To do this, go back to the Skype main window and click on **Contacts** and **Search for Skype Users**.

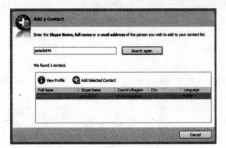

Fig. 2

131

Action 3

If they already use Skype their details will be displayed (Fig. 2). Double click on their name to verify their personal details then click **Close**. Next click on **Add Selected Contact** to add them to your address book.

Fig. 3

Action 4

Finally you'll see the authorisation form (Fig. 3). This confirms you wish to send a message to the person asking if they would like to be in your address book. They can choose to accept or decline. If they accept, their name will appear in your contacts address book in the main Skype window.

If your friend isn't yet using Skype you can click on **Tools**, **Share Skype with a Friend**. This will send an e-mail encouraging them to download the software and get connected so you can add them to your address book.

Non-Skype Contacts
If you want to add a contact who doesn't use Skype but just has a normal telephone, you can do this using a service called SkypeOut. Find out more in Section 8 of this chapter.

Receiving Contacts
Similarly, when your friends add you to their address book a message will pop up asking you if you want to accept. If you block it, they won't be able to call you in the future.

EXPERT TIP
If you change your mind and decide to block a contact you've previously accepted in your address book, or if you want to talk to a friend you've blocked, you can edit your list of blocked contacts. To do this go to **Contacts** then choose **Manage Blocked Users**.

Section 6:
Online Status

Essential Information
Just like instant messaging you and your contacts have an online status. This tells everyone if you're online and available to talk. A small green tick next to a contact's name,

means that they are online and you can call them. To check or change your online status select the arrow next to the green tick at the bottom left of the Skype main window (Fig. 4). For example, you can choose to be **Offline** or **Not Available** if you do not want to talk.

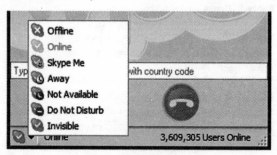

Fig. 4

Note the difference between an **Online** status and a **Skype Me** status. With an online status only people you have approved to be added to your address book can call you. With a **Skype Me** status anyone can call you without your prior approval, just by finding you in the Skype worldwide telephone directory. So, only choose this status if you're willing to accept cold calls.

EXPERT TIP

Every time one of your Skype contacts comes online, you'll get a message to let you know. Sometimes you will be busy and won't want these messages to interrupt you. To switch them off go to **Tools**, **Options** and **Notifications**. Untick the **Comes Online** box.

Section 7:
Making a Call

Action 1
Bring up the Skype main window and click on the contact you wish to call.

Action 2
Click on the green phone button at the bottom of the Skype main window (shown on the left in Fig. 5) or right click on your mouse over the contact's name and select **Start Call** from the drop-down list. The call will connect and start ringing.

Fig. 5

Action 3
When your friend picks up, you can start talking. Their name will appear in the centre of the screen along with the current duration of the call. If you're talking to someone who also uses Skype (as opposed to someone with just a normal telephone number) there are no charges. You can talk for as long as you want for free.

Action 4
You'll find some clever extra options to allow you to interact with the person you are talking to. During the

conversation, right click the name of the person you are talking to and you'll see a list of options (Fig. 6). You can put the call on hold, send written messages to your friend or send a photo or file (Fig. 7), just like with instant messaging.

Fig. 6

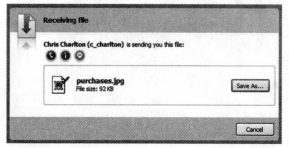

Fig. 7

Action 5

When you've had enough of talking click on the red button at the bottom of the window to end the call (Fig. 5).

EXPERT TIP

If you and your friend have webcams, you'll also be able to see as well as hear each other (Fig. 8). It's the next best thing to actually being there.

Fig. 8

Section 8:
Making a Call with SkypeOut

Essential Information

Skype is great if you know someone else who also uses the program, as you can talk to each other for free. But what if you want to call someone who doesn't use Skype and has a normal telephone, or perhaps doesn't have a computer at all? This is easy with a service called SkypeOut.

SkypeOut allows you to call normal telephones or mobile phones at home or abroad. You have to pay but it can be over 40 per cent cheaper per minute than calling from a normal landline. In order to do this you have to buy euro credits (using your credit card) from the Skype website. For the most popular countries you pay just one fixed rate, called the Skype Global rate.

Action 1

To buy credits go to **File**, **My Skype Account** and then **Go To My Account Page**, or go online and visit skype.com/store. Login using your Skype user name and password and click on **Buy Skype Credit**. It's perfectly secure and you can revisit your account page to top up when you run out of credit. You can also see the latest rates to call countries all over the world.

Action 2

Back on the Skype main window you can see how much credit you have remaining in the top right of the screen (Fig. 9).

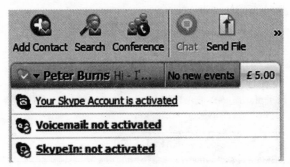

Fig. 9

Action 3

With enough credit you're ready to make a SkypeOut call. Select the **Dial** tab and click on the numbered keypad to dial the number you wish to call (Fig. 10). Push the green telephone button (Fig. 5) to connect.

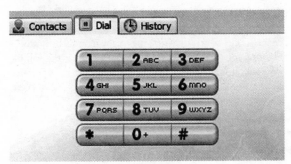

Fig. 10

Action 4

The call will connect and ring. When the person at the other end picks up you can start talking. Remember to keep an eye on the duration as this time you're paying for the call. Click on the red button at the bottom to end the call. You should be aware that because you are calling a normal telephone you won't be able to use many of the additional options such as sending a photo or file to the caller.

EXPERT TIP

Skype is a great way to make calls at low cost or for free but the one thing it can't do is make calls to the emergency services. Make sure you've got another phone at home for emergencies, such as your mobile.

Section 9:
Receiving a Call

Essential Information

With Skype, taking a call from a friend is just as easy as making one. When they call, the Skype icon at the bottom right of your screen will flash. You'll also hear the sound of a telephone ringing. Double click the icon to open up Skype. Once it's open you'll see who is calling and you can choose either to accept or reject the call.

Section 10:
SkypeIn and Voice-mail

Essential Information
SkypeOut lets you call friends who have a normal telephone. However, you'll need SkypeIn if someone with a normal telephone wants to call you. With SkypeIn you get your own telephone number so people with normal phones can call you and you can answer with Skype.

Action 1
To buy a SkypeIn number and Voice-mail account, login in to your account by clicking on **File**, **My Skype Account** and then **Go To My Account Page**, or you can access it on the web at skype.com/store.

Action 2
Select **Get SkypeIn Number** and follow the on-screen instructions to buy your number. You have to choose where your SkypeIn number is based. You can choose any country. If you base your number in London and your neighbours in the next street call, they pay local call rates. If your aunt who lives in Australia calls, she dials the same number but pays international rates. You could also base your number in Australia, meaning that your aunt will pay local rates but your London neighbours pay for international calls. You can even choose a telephone number based on your favourite series of numbers. Fig. 11 shows an example of a UK-based SkypeIn number.

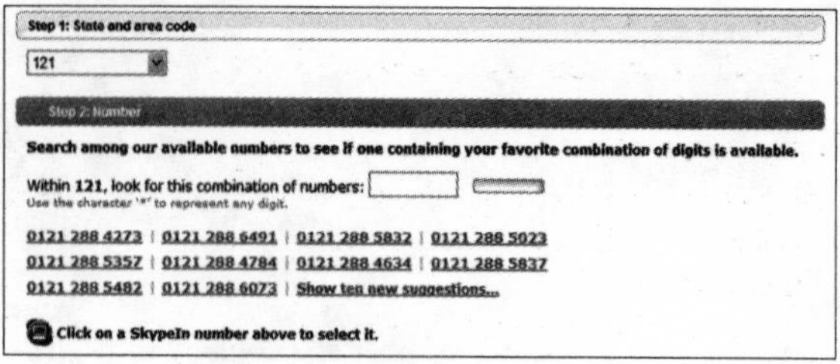

Fig. 11

EXPERT TIP

You can buy and use up to ten SkypeIn numbers. You might want different numbers for home or a small business, or use a local number when you are in another country.

Action 3

If you're not online when you receive a call to your SkypeIn number, the caller can leave you a voice-mail and you can pick it up next time you're online. Any new voice messages appear on the Skype main window the next time you login. Click on **Play** to listen to your message. SkypeIn numbers and voice-mail accounts aren't free but they are much cheaper than the cost of having a normal home telephone as you don't have to pay expensive line rental charges.

EXPERT TIP

You can change the time it takes before your voice-mail starts, if you don't answer a call. Go to **Tools**, **Voice-mail** and enter the time in seconds.

Call Forwarding

If you're away from your computer but still want to take calls you can set up call forwarding instead of voice-mail. This forwards calls to any other number you choose such as your mobile or work phone. You can even forward calls to up to three numbers at once so you'll never miss an important call.

You don't have to buy SkypeIn or Voice-mail to use call forwarding. Anyone with Skype can use it and you simply pay the cost of the call to the number you forward to. To activate it, go to **Tools**, **Call Forwarding** and enter the numbers you want your calls forwarded to.

Section 11:
Conference Calls

Essential Information

Talking to more than one person is much easier with Skype than using a standard telephone. You can talk to up to four people at once, whether they are a Skype user or a contact with a normal telephone number.

Action 1

Select Tools and then Create a Conference Call to get started.

Action 2

You'll see the Conference Call window (Fig. 12). Select a topic for your call (such as 'Meeting up this weekend') and then **Add** up to four contacts from the list on the left to take part in the call.

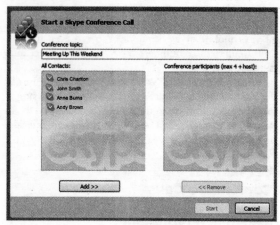

Fig. 12

Action 3

Choose **Start** and Skype will contact all those on the list. After a few seconds everyone should be connected and you can start talking.

Action 4

To end the call press the red button at the bottom of the window.

Section 12:
Personalising Skype

Make Skype more fun by personalising it with your own photo or ringtones.

Action 1
Select **File** and **Edit My Profile**. Enter your personal details here. This makes it easier for your friends to find you in the Skype worldwide telephone directory, but remember; anyone can see these details. However, they won't be able to see your personal e-mail address and if you get an invitation to be added to someone's address book and you don't know who they are, you can (and probably should) reject it.

Action 2
Make sure you add your **Full name** on the **Edit My Profile** page. This is different to your Skype user name. It is the name your friends will see in their own Skype address books.

Action 3
Add a picture of yourself that friends will see when they call you. To do this, click on the **Change** button on the **Edit My Profile** page. Then click on **Browse** to select a picture from your computer. Click on **Update** to finish.

Action 4

From the Skype main window, click on the arrow to the left of your name and you can see your picture and add a personal message that your friends will see (Fig. 13).

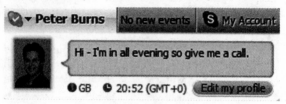

Fig. 13

Action 5

Try personalising your ringtone or other sounds. You can change any of the sounds Skype uses to your own by going to **Tools**, **Options** and then clicking on **Sounds**. Click on the icons on the right to choose a sound file from your own computer.

EXPERT TIP

The sound might be one you record yourself – a quick hello or a welcome greeting. To record your own sound, use Windows Sound Recorder. You'll find this free little tool in the **Accessories** and **Entertainment** folder. Make sure you save your recording in 'WAV' file format. If you don't want to record your own sound you could download one from an Internet sounds website such as altavista. com/audio or findsounds.com.

Section 13:
Getting Help

Skype is designed to be easy to use but if you do experience problems, check out the Skype support website at support. skype.com. You can also chat to other Skype users and get more ideas and help at share.skype.com.

Chapter Nine:
E-mail and Digital Photography

Section 1:
Sending E-mail with Broadband

Essential Information

Sending an e-mail with broadband is no different to sending an e-mail with a normal Internet connection, except you can send much larger files and attachments. This is important as you use your broadband connection more, especially if you're sending music tracks, video clips or photos from your digital camera.

You'll need an e-mail provider first of all. Choose one of the many e-mail accounts that come free from your Internet provider when you register for broadband or sign up for a free webmail account such as Microsoft Hotmail (hotmail.com), Yahoo! Mail (mail.yahoo.co.uk) or Google Gmail (gmail.google.com).

Section 2:
E-mail Attachment Limits

Essential Information

E-mail providers put a limit on the size of the files you can send or attach so their systems don't get overloaded. Broadband lets you easily download large files but e-mail providers don't make it easy to share them because of these restrictions. Fortunately there are a number of things you can do.

Action 1

Find out the maximum attachment size that your e-mail provider will allow, by visiting their website. As e-mail providers are in competition with each other, they increase the limits regularly. If you have a free webmail account such as Hotmail, Yahoo! Mail or Google Gmail you will be limited to sending attachments of 10 MB in size.

Action 2

Find out how much overall storage space there is in your e-mail account. This is the space you have to store all your e-mails and attachments. For example, Hotmail gives you 250 MB, Yahoo! Mail gives you 1 GB and Google Gmail gives you 2 GB. Larger storage space means that you don't have to regularly clear out your e-mail account when sending large files.

Section Three:
Upgrading Your E-mail Account

Essential Information

You can be prevented from sending an e-mail with a large attachment for two reasons: the attachment is too big and your e-mail provider won't let you attach it or the recipient's e-mail system thinks the attachment is too big, and sends you an e-mail saying it has been rejected. What can you do?

Most webmail services offer premium accounts that allow you to send bigger e-mail attachments. Microsoft Hotmail and Yahoo! Mail offer you a large 20 MB attachment limit for a small annual fee. Visit their websites to register and pay. This may sort out your problems but if the person you're e-mailing has a lower attachment limit, you'll still be unable to get large e-mails to them.

Section 4:
Large Attachments and Outlook Express

Essential Information

Outlook Express is one of the most popular e-mail programs and is included in Microsoft Office, the word-processing and spreadsheet software package, although it can be bought from computer retailers.

If you use Outlook Express version 6 or above, it has a clever feature that will automatically split large attachments and send them as separate e-mails. It then reassembles them automatically at the other end. You'll need to be sure the person at the other end also uses Outlook Express otherwise what they receive will make no sense.

Action 1

To switch on this feature, start Outlook Express and click on **Tools** followed by **Accounts**.

Action 2

Choose **Mail, Properties**, click on **Advanced** and tick the box that says **Break apart messages larger than** (Fig. 1). Enter the e-mail attachment limit for your e-mail provider. You have to enter this in kilobytes so you would enter 10,000 for a 10-MB limit. Click **OK** to finish. Outlook Express will then manage sending and receiving large attachments for you.

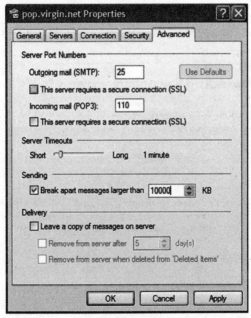

Fig. 1

Section 5:
Large Attachments and Instant Messaging

Instant messaging is like e-mail but allows you to talk in real time. It's also a great option for sending large files as there is virtually no attachment limit. As an added bonus it gives you the chance to chat with the person you're sending it to at the same time. Find out how to use instant messaging in Chapter Four.

Section 6:
Uploading Large Attachments

Essential Information
The final option for sending large e-mail attachments is to post or upload your file to a website page on the Internet. You can then send your friend a simple text e-mail with the website link from where they can download the attachment.

If you're e-mailing a large video clip you could use one of the video e-mail services described in Chapter Seven or try Yahoo! Briefcase. This is a file storage website that allows you to post attachments of up to 30 MB in size to your own personal webpage which friends can then visit to download your files. Register for free at briefcase.yahoo. co.uk and follow the on-screen instructions to upload your files. For even larger attachments, try another file storage website such as Dropload. With Dropload you can upload a file of up to 100 MB in size, and it sends an e-mail to the recipient with a link to the webpage from where it can be downloaded.

Action 1

Log on to dropload.com. Click on **Sign up now** and enter your details to create a free account. Tick the box that gives you virus protection for your attachments.

Action 2

Login to the website with your new user name and password. Enter the e-mail address of the recipient, a message and then click **Browse** to select the file on your computer that you wish to attach (Fig. 2).

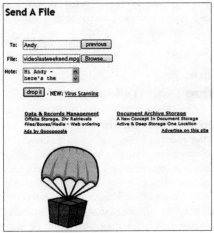

Fig. 2

Action 3

Click on **Drop it** and your file will upload to the Internet and the recipient will receive an e-mail letting them know that the files are available to be downloaded. They have seven days to do so before it gets deleted.

You'll find similar file storage websites at znail.com and sendfile.com.

EXPERT TIP

Another option is to squash your attachment into a smaller file size using compression software. The two most popular are WinZip (winzip.com) and Stuffit Expander (stuffit.com), both of which can be used for free.

They're a good option if your attachment is, for example, 12 MB in size. You can then compress it to squeeze out a few MB and get it under the 10-MB limit. However, for much larger attachments you won't be able to compress it enough. In addition, the person receiving the attachment must have the same software to decompress it.

Section 7:
Sharing Digital Photos

Essential Information

You'll find plenty of digital cameras to choose from at online electrical stores such as Amazon (amazon.co.uk) and each will come with its own software to load photos onto your computer. But for many people that's all they do. The photos sit on their PC and don't go anywhere.

A weekend or trip away with family or friends lasts longer when you share your photos. With broadband you can capture everything with your digital camera and then share the photos online. It's easy to do and is a great reminder of your time together.

The best way to share your digital photos is to use a dedicated photo sharing website such as Flickr.

EXPERT TIP

Before you start sharing your digital photos get them in order with one of these two free software packages: Google Picasa lets you sort your photos, alter them and add captions (picasa.google.com); Adobe Photoshop Album Starter Edition (adobe.com/photoshopalbum) works in a similar way.

Action 1

Flickr is the perfect place for photo sharing and has lots of extra features. To get started visit flickr.com and click **Sign up now** for a free account. If you already have an account with the website Yahoo! (who own Flickr) you can use the same registration details.

Action 2

Choose the option to **Upload** photos (Fig. 3). You can upload up to 20 MB worth of photos a month. If you need to upload more you'll have to register for a premium account and pay a small fee. When you upload your photos, select whether you want them to be public or private. Public photos can be seen by anyone, private photos are for only those people you nominate. You can also select completely private photos so only you can view them. You then have the option to add a description of each photo to complete the upload.

Fig. 3

Action 3

To share your photos go to **Your Account** page and choose **Set up your URL**. This allows you to create your own webpage where your photos will be displayed. E-mail the address of this webpage to your family or friends and they can visit it to see the photos (Fig. 4).

Fig. 4

Action 4

Flickr also allows you to create group listings. You'll find the link to group listings in **Your Account**. A group can be anyone: your family, football team, parents' group or neighbours. The people you nominate can then add photos to the group webpage whenever they like. It's perfect for gatherings like weddings. Set up a group webpage in advance of the big day and after it's all over, each guest who took pictures with a digital camera can upload them for everyone to enjoy.

You'll find other free photo sharing websites at MSN Spaces (spaces.msn.com) or Yahoo! Photos (photos.yahoo.co.uk).

Section 8:
E-mailing Digital Photos

Essential Information
Another way to share your digital photos is by e-mailing them to your friends as an attachment. This can make your e-mail too big so try the ideas in Sections 3 to 6 of this chapter to squash them. Alternatively, Windows XP has an easy way to make your photos small enough to e-mail.

Action 1
Click on the **Start** button on your desktop and choose **My Pictures**. Then find the folder with the photo(s) you want to send and select it using the left mouse button.

Action 2
In the **File and Folder Tasks** box on the left choose the option marked **E-mail this folder's file** (Fig. 5). The **Send Pictures via E-mail** box will pop up. Select **Make all my pictures smaller**. You can specify how much smaller by clicking on **Show more options**. Then click **OK**.

Fig. 5

Action 3

Windows will then automatically launch your e-mail program such as Outlook Express and open up a new e-mail with your pictures attached. All you need to do is add the recipients' e-mail addresses and click **Send**.

Section 9:
Printing Digital Photos

Essential Information

There are two ways you can print your own digital photos. Either at home using your printer, or using an online photography shop. Printing your photos at home can be fun, but by the time you've bought paper and printer ink, it is often faster and less expensive to upload your photos to an online shop and have them posted to you.

Printing Photos at Home

To print photos at home you'll need a good quality ink jet or laser printer, the correct paper and software. For everyday photos, use standard inkjet paper with 360 dpi (dots per inch). This shows how much ink the paper can absorb. The higher the number, the better quality of printing you'll receive.

For a more professional result choose special photographic paper, though it is more expensive. This can be gloss or matt finish and should be 'instant dry' to prevent colour running. Make sure you choose paper of the correct weight (measured in gsm). A weight of between 160 and 200 gsm should be fine, although if you want the same quality as a retail photo developer, choose 280 gsm.

The quality of home photo printing depends a lot on the quality of your printer. Advanced photographers can get an optimal result by adjusting the colour of their photos using software. You can make basic adjustments using Google Picasa or Adobe Photoshop Album (see Section 7 of this chapter) or use advanced software such as Adobe Photoshop (adobe.com/photoshop) or Paint Shop Pro (corel.co.uk).

However, you don't need additional software to print basic photos. Windows XP can print them for you.

Action 1

Open your **My Pictures** folder or the folder where you keep your photographs. Click on the **Print Pictures** link on the left. This will start the Photo Printing Wizard.

Action 2

Click **Next** and then choose the photos you wish to print by placing a tick in the box next to each one (Fig. 6).

Action 3

Choose which printer you wish to use and click **Next**.

Action 4

Select the layout of how you want the photos printed. For example, one or two per page. Finally, click **Next** to start printing.

Fig. 6

Online Photography Shops

There are lots of online photography shops you can choose from. These differ from the photo sharing websites in Section 7 as they will also print and mail your photos to you. In the US, popular stores include Yahoo! Photos (photos.yahoo.com) and Shutterfly (shutterfly.com). In the UK try the award-winning PhotoBox.

Action 1

To order prints visit photobox.com and register by clicking on the **Join Free** link at the top of the page.

Action 2

Once you're registered, login with your user name and password and select **Create Album**. All photos are stored in albums and can be set up to store photos from a weekend break or holiday. Give your album a name and description and then choose **Save this album and upload photos to it now**.

Action 3

You'll be given the option to choose which photos on your computer you want to upload. Browse to your photo folder on your computer and click on the photos you want. If you're uploading lots of photos hold down the **CTRL** key on your keyboard as you click on each one. Click **OK** to finish.

Action 4

Back on the PhotoBox webpage, choose **Start Upload** to add your photos to your album. If you have a lot of photos the upload can take some time even with broadband, so be patient.

Action 5

You'll see all your photos in the **My Albums** part of PhotoBox (Fig. 7). From here you can click on **Print all photos** to order them to be delivered to your home or to someone else as a gift. You don't just have to send photos. You can turn them in to all sorts of things such as calendars, stickers, posters or a slideshow disc for your DVD player.

Fig. 7

EXPERT TIP

If you're a budding professional photographer, PhotoBox also has excellent Professional Photo Galleries. Register for an account as usual but set up a **Pro Gallery** instead. You can set a price for each of your photos and sell them using PhotoBox's secure payment system. It is used by large companies as well as thousands of amateur photographers.

Chapter Ten:
Wireless at Home

Section 1:
Benefits of Wireless

Essential Information

Wireless or 'Wi-Fi' Internet (Wi-Fi stands for wireless fidelity) enables you to enjoy broadband without wires, by transmitting your Internet connection as radio waves to your computer. Wi-Fi enables you to surf the web anywhere in your home and gives you the freedom to do a lot more with your computer, such as:

- Browse the latest news online instead of buying a newspaper.
- Take breakfast in the garden whilst listening to your favourite radio shows online.
- In the kitchen, use your laptop to discover new recipe ideas.
- Chat to your friends online in the lounge, kitchen or study.
- Download a film and watch it anywhere in the house.

Section 2:
Wireless Home Networks

Essential Information

With home Wi-Fi, you can connect your broadband service to just one computer or to several. Wi-Fi is best with a laptop, but you can also use it with a desktop computer.

Laptops

If you have just one laptop, Wi-Fi gives you the freedom to go online anywhere in your home. If you have more than one they can be connected together to share your broadband connection.

Desktops

If you have a desktop computer and a laptop, Wi-Fi can connect them together. For example, you may have a desktop in the kids' bedroom and a laptop in your study. Wi-Fi can also connect two desktop computers together if they are in different rooms of the house.

Networks

Connecting more than one desktop or laptop together creates a 'home network'. A home network allows each computer to share the same folders, Internet connection and even printer (Fig. 1). A home network is also called a LAN (Local Area Network). They can be connected using wires, but wireless home networks (or WLANs) mean that you don't have to hide network cables under carpets or in walls.

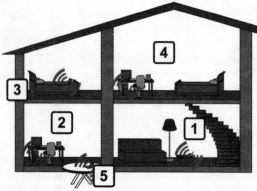

Fig. 1

Section 3:
Wireless Standards

Essential Information

To create a wireless home network you'll need to buy extra equipment (it can be found at any computer store). But before you do so, you need to choose which wireless standard to use. A wireless standard describes the type of radio waves used to transmit your broadband signal through your home. There are two home wireless standards to choose from.

Wireless B

Also known as 802.11b, this is the most common standard and is good for connecting together one or two computers. This is the same standard used in coffee shops and airports (see Chapter Eleven for more about wireless on the move). However, you might find watching live video on your laptop to be a little jerky.

Wireless G

Also known as 802.11g and five times faster than Wireless B, this is a more recent standard and is great for watching lots of live video. Choose this standard if you will be using your laptop all over a big house, or if you'll be connecting several computers together and will often have people using them simultaneously. If you, your partner and the kids are all online at once, it won't slow down the speed of your network.

EXPERT TIP

Whether you go for Wireless B or Wireless G, buy equipment with the same standard (and preferably from the same manufacturer). If you buy Wireless G equipment, it's also compatible with Wireless B.

Section 4:
Two Ways to Go Wireless

You can create a wireless home network in one of two ways. For each one you'll need different equipment.

Ad-hoc

This is the easiest way to go wireless if you have two or more computers. You'll need at least one desktop computer with broadband connected to your telephone or cable service as normal using a modem. The desktop computer then wirelessly connects to all the other computers in your home. The other computers can be all laptops, desktops, or a combination of the two. (Fig. 2).

All you need for an ad-hoc network is a wireless adapter for your desktop and for each of your other computers (wireless adapters are explained in Section 6 of this chapter).

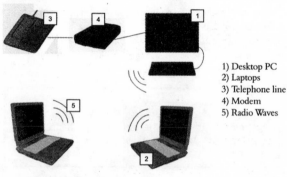

1) Desktop PC
2) Laptops
3) Telephone line
4) Modem
5) Radio Waves

Fig. 2

Infrastructure

This is the option to use if you don't have a desktop computer but have one or more laptops you wish to use without wires. This requires a router. A router is a box that takes the Internet connection from your modem and converts it into radio waves to transmit throughout your home (Fig. 3).

For this type of set up you'll need a modem and a separate router although you can use a combined modem/router as shown in Fig. 3. You'll also need wireless adapters for each of your laptops.

1) Laptops
2) Telephone line
3) Modem
4) Radio Waves

Fig. 3

Section 5: Routers

Essential Information

A typical router looks like the image in Fig. 4. There are two types of router you can buy depending on what type of modem you have. If you have an Ethernet or USB modem you'll need an Ethernet or USB compatible router to match.

Fig. 4

Action 1

To find out which type of broadband modem you have, look at the back of it. If it has a thin oblong slot about half an inch wide or square in a similar shape to the outline of a house, you have a USB modem. If it is square like a telephone socket you have an Ethernet modem. Some modems have both sockets (as in Fig. 5) so you can choose whichever router you want.

Fig. 5

If you need to buy a router you may want to consider replacing your modem with a combined modem/wireless router. Make sure you buy wireless equipment, as you can also buy combined modem/routers for wired networks. Ask your Internet provider if they can provide one when you first sign up for broadband.

EXPERT TIP

You'll find several manufacturers of wireless equipment which you can buy in your local computer or electronics store, or online from companies such as Amazon. Reliable brand names to look out for are Belkin, Buffalo, D-Link, Linksys and NETGEAR.

Section 6:
Wireless Adapters

Essential Information

You'll need a wireless adapter for each of the computers you'll be connecting together. A router transmits your broadband connection as radio waves and the wireless adapter receives the incoming radio waves. You'll also need an adapter for your printer if you wish to share it amongst all the computers in your network.

Action 1

Check first if you already have a wireless adapter in each of your computers. Right click on the **My Computer** icon on the desktop and then select **Properties**. Click the **Hardware** tab and then the **Device Manager** button. If you have a wireless adapter it will be listed in the **Network Adapters** option. The majority of modern laptops come with wireless adaptors built in as standard.

If You Don't Have a Wireless Adapter

If you don't already have a wireless adapter you'll need to buy some and fit them to each of the computers in your home network. The type you buy will depend on whether you have a laptop or a desktop computer.

Laptop

If you have a laptop computer you'll need a **wireless PC card**. It's a small, flat credit-card sized adapter (Fig. 6).

Fig. 6

Desktop

If you have a desktop computer you'll need either a **wireless PCI card** (Fig. 7) or a **USB wireless adapter** (Fig. 8). A wireless PCI card plugs into an empty expansion slot in the back of your computer but you will have to remove the outer case of your computer to connect it. With supplied instructions it's not too complicated but for most people it's a job for your local computer store. It is better to get a USB wireless adapter. Plug this into a spare USB socket on your computer so you don't have to open it up.

Fig. 7

Fig. 8

Section 7:

Connecting a Wireless Network

Once you have the right equipment, connecting everything together should take less than half an hour. You need to follow these four steps:

1. Install your router (if required).
2. Install your wireless adapters.
3. Configure your network.
4. Secure your network.

Section 8:
Installing a Router

You'll need to do this if you're setting up an infrastructure network. If you wish to create an ad-hoc network or have a combined modem/wireless router already installed, then you can skip this step and go straight to Section 9.

Action 1
Plug your router into your modem. The cables that come with your router will plug into either the Ethernet or USB socket of your modem depending on which type you have.

EXPERT TIP

To ensure your router's signal can reach all parts of your home, place it off the ground. If you have a large house, place it somewhere central to ensure the best signal. Avoid placing it next to metal doors, filing cabinets or electronic devices that use radio waves such as microwave ovens or cordless phones. They will all interfere with your router's signal.

Action 2

Next change the connection settings on each of the computers in your network. Go to **Start**, **Control Panel** then **Network and Internet Connections** and then **Network Connections**. Double click the network connection marked **Local Area Connection** and on the **General** tab select **Properties**. A new window will appear.

Action 3

In the **General** tab of this new window (Fig. 9) double click on **Internet Protocol** from the drop-down list in the centre of the window. Another new window will pop up. Choose **Obtain an IP address automatically** (Fig. 10). Finally click **OK** twice to finish.

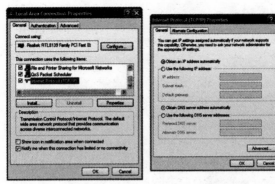

Fig. 9   Fig. 10

EXPERT TIP

With Windows XP, if you cannot see the **Network and Internet Connections** link in Action 2, then you've probably got your system set to **Classic View**. This is the older style of Windows desktop. To change this to the more user friendly **Category View**, click on **Switch to Category View** in the top left of the window.

Action 4

Next you need to configure your router. In your router's user guide there will be a special web address (also called an IP address). Go to any computer in your home network, open the web browser and enter this address.

175

Action 5

When you are asked for a user name and password, enter the user name and password from your router's user guide.

Action 6

You should then see the router online set-up page (Fig. 11). Here you must select the **Internet Connection Type**. For most people this will be **Obtain an IP automatically** (also known as Automatic Configuration). During set-up you will need to enter the user name and password you use to connect to your broadband service. Some Internet providers require you to enter extra information to complete the set-up page. If you have connection problems with your router, you should contact your Internet provider to ask if you need this extra information.

Fig. 11

Section 9:
Installing Wireless Adapters

Action 1

Switch off your computer and plug in your wireless adapter. Switch it back on and if you have Windows XP, your computer will recognise the adapter and start the **Found New Hardware Wizard** (Fig. 12).

Fig. 12

Action 2

Follow the on-screen instructions to complete installation automatically. If you have an older version of Windows you'll need to first insert the CD that came with your adapter and install set-up software before plugging in the adapter.

Action 3

Repeat the above for each laptop or desktop computer in your network.

Section 10:
Configuring an Ad-hoc Wireless Network

Essential Information

If you've decided to create an ad-hoc wireless network and you've installed all your wireless adapters, you now need to configure your computers to talk to each other. Remember, ad-hoc uses an existing desktop computer connected to the Internet and shares the connection with other computers in your home whether they be desktop or laptop.

Action 1

When you installed your wireless adapters you will have been given the choice of using either an ad-hoc or infrastructure network. Make sure you choose ad-hoc. On each of your computers you can go back into the software for your wireless adapter via the **All Programs** menu in Windows to select ad-hoc, if you haven't done so already.

Action 2

Go to your existing desktop computer which is connected to the Internet. In the bottom of your screen you will see the wireless connection icon (Fig. 13).

Fig. 13

178

Right click your mouse over the icon and select **Open Network Connections**.

Action 3

You'll see a list of your Internet and network connections. Right click over the one marked **Wireless Network Connection** and choose **Properties.** Click on the **Wireless Networks** tab (Fig. 14) and then press the **Advanced** button near the bottom of the screen.

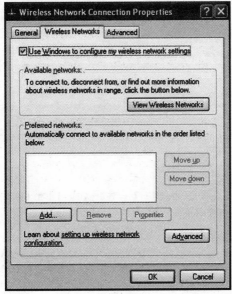

Fig. 14

Action 4

Finally select **Computer-to-computer (ad hoc) networks only** (Fig. 15). Make sure the box marked **Automatically connect to non-preferred networks** is not ticked.

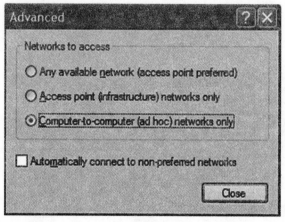

Fig. 15

Action 5

Click back on the **Wireless Networks** tab at the top of the window and select **Add.**

Action 6

Give your network a name (Fig. 16). This is known as the SSID or 'Service Set Identifier'. Enter a name, for example 'Peter Home Network'. Here you can also set security options (these are discussed later in Section 13). Click

OK. You'll see your new network listed with a red cross next to it. This means you need to add other computer(s) such as your laptop to complete the network.

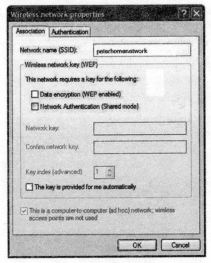

Fig. 16

Action 7

On each of your other computers right click the mouse over the wireless connection icon (Fig. 13) and choose **View Available Wireless Networks**. You should see your new network name listed. Select it and click **OK**.

Action 8

Go back to the desktop computer you first set up and tell Windows to share your Internet connection between all the computers on your network. To do this, click on **Start**, **Control Panel** then **Network Connections**. Select your Internet connection and click on **Change settings of this connection** from the list of Networks Tasks on the left (Fig. 17).

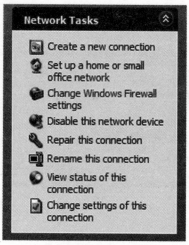

Fig. 17

Action 9

Select the **Advanced** tab and then tick the box that says **Allow other network users to connect through this computer's Internet connection** (Fig. 18).

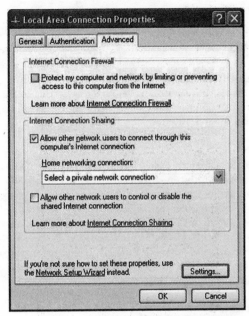

Fig. 18

Action 10

You can now access the Internet wirelessly on any computer in your network by opening your web browser.

Section 11:
Configuring an Infrastructure Wireless Network

Essential Information

For this, you will need a modem and router. Infrastructure is also the option to choose if you have one laptop and want to use it wirelessly around the house.

Action 1

If all the computers in your network have Windows XP you can do this using the **Wireless Network Setup Wizard.** This guides you through configuration and also lets you add new computers to a wireless home network you may have already set up. You'll need to download Windows Service Pack 2 or later, on each computer in order to use the setup wizard. Service Pack 2 is an essential download as it also includes important security patches for your computer. Find out how to get it in Chapter Three.

Action 2

Once you've downloaded and installed Windows Service Pack 2, go to a computer (preferably one already connected to a printer) and click **Start**, **Control Panel**, **Network and Internet Connections** and click on **Wireless Network Setup Wizard** (Fig. 19).

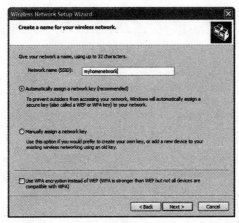

Fig. 19

Action 3

You'll be asked to give your network a unique name (known as the SSID or 'Service Set Identifier').

Action 4

Next the wizard will ask you how you want to set up your network (Fig. 20). You'll be given a choice of using a USB flash drive or doing it manually.

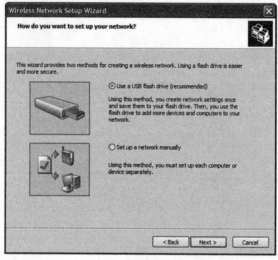

Fig. 20

Action 5

A USB flash drive (Fig. 21) is the easiest way to configure a network and is a small disk drive the size of a keyring. It plugs into the USB socket on your computer and can store and upload files instantly. It's a handy way of carrying files around in your pocket. Flash drives are inexpensive and can be purchased from all computer retailers.

Fig. 21

Plug the drive into the USB socket on your computer and follow the wizard's on-screen instructions. The configuration files for all the computers in your home network will be downloaded to the flash drive. Plug it into the USB socket on your router, each of your computers and your printer (if required).

When you plug the flash drive into your router or printer, the lights on it will flash to let you know it has configured that device. When you plug it into each of your other computers a pop-up window will appear. Select the **Wireless Network Setup Wizard** and follow the on-screen instructions.

Action 6

Finally plug the USB flash drive back into the first computer on which you initially started the wizard and follow the on-screen instructions. Your home network will then be complete.

Manual Setup

If you don't have a USB flash drive you can select to configure your network manually. The wizard will then print out a list of settings, or you can write them down. The settings will include the name of your network and any security codes.

All you need to do is go to the other computers in your home network and right click your mouse over the wireless icon at the bottom of your desktop screen. Choose **View available wireless networks** (follow the instructions in Section 4 of Chapter Eleven to do this). When you try and connect you will be asked for a **network key** (Fig. 22). This will be provided on the printout that the wizard created for you. Enter the key to allow your other computers to access your wireless home network.

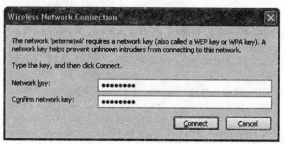

Fig. 22

EXPERT TIP

If your wireless connection stops working you can fix it by right clicking your mouse on the wireless connection icon (Fig. 13) and selecting **Repair**.

Section 12:
Signal Strength

Action 1

The strength of your wireless signal decreases as you move away from your router. The maximum range indoors is approximately 100 metres. Once your network is running, check the signal strength by right clicking on the **wireless connection icon** at the bottom right of your screen and selecting **View available wireless networks**. You'll see your wireless home network listed along with an indication of the network's signal strength (Fig. 23).

Fig. 23

Carefully positioning your router will minimise signal reduction, especially in large homes with lots of walls. If the signal strength drops in the far corners of your home you will need to buy a booster (also known as a 'repeater'). A booster simply plugs into an electrical plug socket in low signal areas, and helps to boost the radio waves from your router so they reach a greater distance. A good choice of booster is the Linksys Range Expander (linksys.com).

EXPERT TIP

To extend the range of your wireless home network, you can buy a router (or wireless laptop adapters) that has a connector to which you can attach an external aerial. The aerial is only small but will help boost the signal range.

Section 13:
Wireless Security

Essential Information

Many people go to the trouble of setting up a wireless home network but don't secure it. This means any neighbour or passer-by in the street with a wireless laptop can find and access your home network.

If you're feeling generous you can leave it unsecured for your neighbours to use. But if you're using a broadband service with usage limits, letting others gain access means that you may reach your monthly limit more quickly. More importantly, an unsecured network makes it easier for hackers to access your computer.

There are five simple steps to get basic security on your wireless home network:

Buy a Router with a Built-in Firewall

A firewall monitors traffic flowing from the Internet to your home network. Check the product specifications of your router to see if it has a built-in firewall. Alternatively you can install a firewall on each of the computers in your home network. See Chapter Three for more on this.

Change the SSID

Your router will have its own default name (SSID). Hackers know what default manufacturer settings are, so you need to change the SSID to prevent them gaining access.

Action 1

In your router's set-up page (Fig. 11) change the SSID to a different name.

Disable the SSID Broadcast

An SSID broadcast sends a signal to nearby computers to tell them you have a wireless network, so it is important to switch it off to keep your network hidden.

Action 1

In your router's set-up page select **Disable SSID broadcast**.

Change Your Router's User Name and Password

On your router set-up page it will also have a default user name and password. Hackers know the default user names and passwords.

Action 1

In your router's administration or security page, enter your own unique user name and password. You'll find the administration or security page during router setup (see Section 8 of this chapter).

Enable WEP Security

WEP stands for Wired Equivalent Privacy and you can ask Windows XP to automatically turn it on. It encrypts your wireless broadband signal to prevent anyone snooping on it.

Action 1

To turn on WEP, tick the box that says **Automatically assign a network key** (Fig. 19) when you start the Wireless Network Setup Wizard.

EXPERT TIP

If you've had your router for a while you can update it by downloading software (also known as 'firmware') from the manufacturer's website.

Section 14:
Advanced Wireless Security

Essential Information

Basic security will be fine for most homes. However, there are three advanced security measures you can take if you want to reduce the chances of anyone getting unauthorised access to your home network.

Action 1

On every wireless device (such as your wireless laptop adapter or router) find the 'Media Access Code' or MAC. It looks just like a serial number and can be found on the outer casing of each device. Next go to your router set-up security page. The exact set-up page will vary depending on which router you have. With a Linksys router, select the button that says **Permit only PCs listed below to access the wireless network**. Next click on the **Edit MAC Filter List** button and enter each MAC code (Fig. 24). This initiates what's known as 'MAC address filtering' or cloning. This means that your wireless home network will only work with the devices that have those specific MAC codes.

MAC Address Filter List

Enter MAC Address in this format: xxxxxxxxxxxx

Wireless Client MAC List

MAC 01:	05:02:20:0h:d2:f4	**MAC 11:**	
MAC 02:	00:55:88:C1:79:DD	**MAC 12:**	
MAC 03:		**MAC 13:**	

Fig. 24

Action 2

You'll also need to enter the MAC address for each of the computers on your network. Click **Start**, **Run** then enter '**command**' in the box and click **OK**. You'll see a new window with a black background. Next type **ipconfig/all** and press the **Enter** key. You'll see a list of network information. Look for the line called **Physical address**.

That's your computer's MAC address. It will consist of a series of numbers and letters.

Action 3

With basic wireless security, you can enable WEP on your network. WPA (Wi-Fi Protected Access) is a more advanced form of encryption. When buying wireless equipment, look to see if it is WPA enabled. If it is then you can turn on advanced encryption by ticking **Use**

WPA encryption instead of WEP in the Wireless Network Setup Wizard (Fig. 19).

EXPERT TIP

If you want advanced security with minimum fuss buy software that will configure and secure your network for you. Download the excellent ZoneAlarm Wireless Security at zonealarm.com, or Wireless Home Network Security at mcafee.com.

Section 15:
Other Wireless Devices

Essential Information

It's not just computers and a printer you can connect wirelessly. You can now buy Wi-Fi compatible devices for your television and music system.

Television

Wireless television adapters allow you to watch video clips or films from your computer on your television. The NETGEAR Wireless Digital Media Player (netgear.co.uk) is a good device to choose.

Music System

Wireless music adapters allow you to send tracks from your computer and listen to them on your music system. Choose a device such as the Linksys Wireless Media Adapter (linksys.com).

You'll also find home media systems that connect your PC to both your TV and your music system. Try the Philips Streamium (streamium.com).

Games Consoles

Consoles such as a Microsoft Xbox or PlayStation allow you to play games against real people in real time over your broadband connection. Visit playstation.com or xbox.com to find out more.

Connecting Other Devices

Connecting these devices to your wireless network is the same as with your computer. Each will come with set-up software that allows you to configure them using either a USB flash card or manually. They then connect to your TV or music system using normal audio and video wires. When buying equipment, Wireless B standard is fine for music, but go for Wireless G for TV, to ensure better-quality video.

Section 16:
Further Help

For further help and advice on wireless set-up and security check out these useful websites:

About
compnetworking.about.com

D-Link
dlink.com/tutorial/wireless

Linksys
linksys.com/learningcenter

Microsoft
microsoft.com/windowsxp/using/networking/default.mspx

NETGEAR
netgear.com/applications

PC Pitstop
pcpitstop.com

Practically Networked
practicallynetworked.com

Section 17:
Other Ways to Go Wireless

There are two alternative ways to create a wireless network in your home:

HomePlug Technology
If you have a large house with thick walls, getting a strong wireless signal in the outer reaches of your home may be troublesome. A solution to this problem is to use a mains network kit.

This connects your router to your nearest electrical plug socket and transmits your broadband connection using the electrical wires that run through your home. Plug an adapter (Fig. 25) into a socket in any other room and your laptop will easily be able to pick up the signal. If you need to move to a different room, unplug the adapter and plug it in somewhere else.

Fig. 25

EXPERT TIP

Try MicroLink's dLAN Starter Kit (devolo.co.uk), NETGEAR's Wall-Plugged Ethernet Bridge (netgear.co.uk) or the Instant PowerLine USB Adapter from linksys.com.

Wireless Broadband Providers

Instead of buying broadband from an Internet provider and then converting it into radio waves in your home with a router, you can buy radio wave broadband directly. A large antenna transmits broadband throughout your local town and into your home using radio waves.

However, such services are in limited areas and have a maximum speed of around 1 Mb. Now (now.com) offers this service in selected areas of the UK. Check your local area to see if there's a similar service near you.

Chapter Eleven:
Wireless on the Move

Section 1:
Wireless Hotspots Explained

Essential Information

Your wireless world doesn't stop when you walk out your front door. There are now hundreds of thousands of wireless or 'Wi-Fi' hotspots around the world that you can use when you're on the move.

A hotspot is a place outside your home that transmits broadband Internet as radio waves. Your laptop can pick up these radio waves to allow you to surf the web. You'll find them in places such as cafés, pubs, shops and airports.

Section 2:
Wireless Adapters

Essential Information

To use wireless hotspots you'll need a laptop computer with a wireless adapter. A wireless adapter receives the radio wave signals from a hotspot, and converts them into an Internet connection for your computer. Most modern laptops come with a built-in wireless adapter so you don't need to buy any extra equipment. They're the best option for using Wi-Fi hotspots if you're thinking of buying a new computer.

Action 1

To check if you already have a wireless adapter in your laptop, right click on the **My Computer** icon on the desktop and select **Properties**. Click the **Hardware** tab and then the **Device Manager** button. If you have a wireless adapter it will be listed in the **Network Adapters** option.

If you don't already have a wireless adapter, you'll need to buy one from any computer or online electronics retailer. It's called a **wireless PC card** and looks like a credit card (Fig. 1). Popular brands you can buy are DLink (dlink.com), Linksys (linksys.com), NETGEAR (netgear.co.uk) and SanDisk (sandisk.com).

Fig. 1

Wireless standards are explained in Chapter Ten. These refer to the type of radio wave signal used by both the hotspot and the wireless adapter. Most hotspots use Wireless B standard so choose a wireless PC card that is Wireless B compatible. Some hotspots use the much faster Wireless G standard. Wireless G works with all types of hotspot. It will cost you more to buy but if you happen to find a hotspot that uses Wireless G, you can connect to the web at incredibly fast speeds.

Action 2

Plug the wireless PC card into the PC card expansion slot on your laptop (you'll find this at the back or on the side). Your laptop will recognise it automatically and will display a **Found New Hardware** message. Insert the software CD-ROM that comes with your PC card and follow the on-screen instructions to complete the set up.

EXPERT TIP

If you don't have a spare PC card expansion slot, you can buy a USB wireless adapter. It does the same job as a PC card, you just plug it into the USB socket on your laptop instead.

Handheld Computers

Alternatively, you can use handheld computers or Pocket PCs, such as the Palm LifeDrive Mobile Manager (palm.com) or the HP iPAQ with Wi-Fi (hp.com). If you're buying a handheld computer, check in the product specification, that it has Wi-Fi hotspot compatibility or look for the 'Wi-Fi certified' logo. Finding and connecting to hotspots with a handheld computer is done in much the same way as connecting with a laptop.

EXPERT TIP

If you have an older handheld computer that isn't Wi-Fi certified, you may be able to add Wi-Fi if it has a compact flash expansion slot. You can check if it has one by looking at the instruction manual. Expansion slots allow you to add extra features to your handheld by plugging a suitable card into the slot. If you have a compact flash slot you can buy a Wi-Fi card. SanDisk (sandisk.com) and Linksys (linksys.com) make Wi-Fi compact flash cards, or you could ask your local computer retailer for their recommendations. Alternatively, consider upgrading to a new handheld which is Wi-Fi certified.

Section 3:
Types of Hotspot

Once you have the right equipment, the next step is to know how to find a hotspot when you're on the move. There are two types of hotspot – fee paying or free.

Fee Paying Hotspots
Most hotspots are fee based and are run by major hotspot networks, such as T-Mobile. If you intend to use wireless hotspots a lot, you can sign up for an account in advance and pay a monthly or annual fee. If you're more likely to be an occasional user or use hotspots from different networks, it is better to sign up for a Pay As You Go account when you next visit each hotspot. These can be paid on an hourly or per minute basis.

Free Hotspots
You can find free hotspots too. Some cafés or pubs offer free hotspots to encourage you to visit their premises in the hope you will buy something.

EXPERT TIP
If you're in a big city you will often be able to access other peoples' wireless networks from nearby homes or businesses. If you do find one, it may be because they are happy for other people to use their network for free, or it may be because they have failed to secure it properly. There's nothing to stop you using it if you want to surf the web. Chapter Ten explains how important it is to secure your home wireless network.

Section 4:
Finding a Hotspot

Essential Information

You'll find hotspots all over the world. You're more likely to find one in a town and there are a lot to choose from in the UK and the US. The easiest way to find a hotspot is to search for one in an online directory before you leave home (see Section 5 of this chapter). But if you're already out and need to find one, your laptop will tell you if there's one nearby (within 70–100 metres).

Action 1

To see if you are in a hotspot area, switch on your laptop. Place your mouse over the wireless network connection icon in the bottom right of your laptop screen (Fig. 2) and right click it.

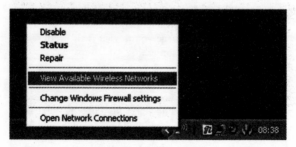

Fig. 2

Action 2

Click **View available wireless networks**. Here you will see the Wireless Network Connection window. If there are any hotspots in your area their names will be listed here. If you're in Starbucks for example, you'll see **T-Mobile** as the network listed. Click on it and select **Connect**. Your laptop is now connected to the hotspot (Fig. 3). Open up your Internet browser (such as Internet Explorer) and follow the on-screen instructions in Section 7 of this chapter to get online.

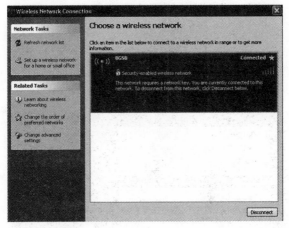

Fig. 3

EXPERT TIP

If you don't use Windows XP, you can download free software from the Internet that searches for hotspots and alerts you if it finds one. NetStumbler is a popular choice and can be downloaded from netstumbler.com. Your wireless PC card may also come with software that does this for you or some of the hotspot networks (such as boingo.com) have hotspot-searching software you can download.

Action 3

If there isn't a hotspot listed in the Wireless Network Connection window, you'll need to find one. In large cities it is not uncommon to simply walk down the street for just ten minutes to find a hotspot signal.

Large Stores and Hotels

Big chain hotels and stores also offer wireless hotspots in many of their locations and are a good place to go if you're looking for a hotspot. Some of the biggest to look out for are:

Borders

bordersstores.co.uk

BT Openzone Payphones

www.btopenzone.com

Caffè Nero

caffenero.com

McDonald's
mcdwireless.com

Starbucks
starbucks.com

Hilton Hotels
hilton.com

Holiday Inn Express
hiexpress.com

Section 5:
Hotspot Directories

Essential Information
The easiest way to find a hotspot is to check out a list of them in the area you will be visiting before you leave home. You can do this online using one of the following hotspot directories. Simply enter your town in the search box and you'll be presented with a list of hotspots (Fig. 4). You can print out the results to take with you or better still, many will give you the option to download the locations to your laptop so you can refer to the list any time you want.

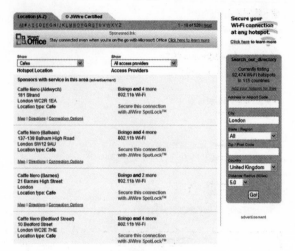

Fig. 4

The HotSpot Haven

hotspothaven.com

The HotSpot Directory

hotspot-hotel.com

Jiwire

jiwire.com

Total Hotspots

totalhotspots.com

WiFi411
wifi411.com

Wi-Fi Hotspot List
wi-fihotspotlist.com

WiFinder
wifinder.com

Wi-Fi Zone
wi-fizone.org

WiFi Free Spot
wififreespot.com

EXPERT TIP

Another useful way to find a hotspot near you is to use Google Local. This is a local online information service that indicates shops and businesses on an easy-to-read map so you can see exactly where to go.

To access this website visit local.google.co.uk (or local.google.com in the US), enter your location name or postcode and hit **Search**. You'll then see a map of your area. Now search again on **Wi-Fi**, and nearby hotspots will appear on the map.

Section 6:
Hotspot Finding Gadgets

Essential Information

The problem with walking down the street to find a hotspot, is that you'll need to keep taking your laptop out of its bag to see if there is a hotspot nearby. A useful gadget to buy is a handheld hotspot finder (Fig. 5). This can be used as a keyring and has a hotspot button on it. Press the button at any time and it will tell you if there is a hotspot nearby. Two good finders are the Kensington WiFi Finder (kensington.com) or the Trust WiFi Hot Spot Finder (trust.com).

Fig. 5

Section 7:
Using a Hotspot

Once you've found a hotspot and are connected to it you're ready to go online.

Action 1

Open your Internet browser such as Internet Explorer. If you're in a free hotspot you'll see a web page for the café, shop or wherever you are. You can then surf the web as normal.

Action 2

If you're in a fee-paying hotspot you'll see a webpage for the hotspot network such as BT Openzone (Fig. 6). Click to buy an e-voucher with your credit card to start using the hotspot, or enter your login details if you already have an account with that network. You're then ready to surf.

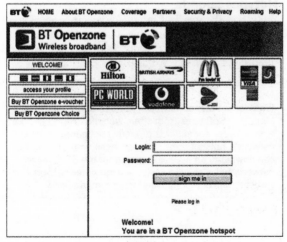

Fig. 6

Action 3

If you choose a Pay As You Go account, it will last for a set number of hours. Don't forget to keep an eye on how long you've been online to keep the cost down. Try doing so by using a simple online alarm clock. Search for free downloadable alarm clocks at download.com.

Action 4

Make sure you log off from your account and then close your web browser when you've finished, to ensure that you don't use any more of the credit in your account.

Hotspot Speeds

You'll find the speed of Internet access in a hotspot is as good as your access at home. But as everyone in that hotspot shares an Internet connection, you may find the speed slows down in very busy hotspot locations.

EXPERT TIP

With some hotspot networks you can download Access Manager Software from their website (Fig. 7). This ensures your computer is properly configured for all the network's hotspots and you can easily get online. You can download an access manager for the BT Openzone network that also works with several other networks at www.btopenzone.com/using/access_manager.

Fig. 7

Section 8:
Hotspot Networks

You'll find at least one of these networks to be operating hotspots in locations near you. You can register for an account in advance or when you're next at a hotspot.

Boingo
boingo.com

BT Open Zone
www.btopenzone.com

T-Mobile
t-mobile.co.uk/hotspot in the UK or t-mobile.com/hotspot in the US

The Cloud
www.thecloud.net

Wayport
wayport.net (US only)

Section 9:
Hotspot Security

Essential Information

Ensuring your Internet activity is secure is even more important when you're on the move. (See Chapter Ten for more on how to secure a wireless network at home and prevent anyone else connecting to it.) But public hotspots do want you to connect to them and as a result have much lower levels of security.

You're most at risk of a hacker attack when you're using a hotspot. Hackers use hotspots to snoop on your wireless signal or trap you in an 'evil twin' hotspot. Evil twins are so called because the hacker sits nearby and creates a second hotspot that tricks you into thinking it is actually the location's hotspot. Once you connect to the evil twin the hacker can spy on your Internet activity.

You need to take these seven steps to stay safe when using a Wi-Fi hotspot:

Action 1

Make sure you have a firewall on your laptop, use up-to-date anti-virus software and use Windows Update regularly. Find out how to do this in Chapter Three.

Action 2

Choose a hotspot that has advanced security such as one of the major networks rather than one in a local shop or café. If the hotspot advertises itself as offering Wi-Fi Protected Access or 'WPA' it has better security.

Action 3

It's fine to check your e-mail account when you're in a hotspot but save any sensitive jobs, such as accessing your online bank account, until you get home.

Action 4

Make sure you are using a secure website when you enter your credit card details online in a hotspot. Look for the little padlock symbol at the bottom of your browser window (Fig. 8).

Fig. 8

Action 5

Switch off file and print sharing. This is a setting that shares the files on your computer with other people using the same wireless network. If you are using a public hotspot, it's not wise to share your files with anyone. To switch this off, go to **Start**, **Control Panel**, then **Network and Internet Connections** and select **Network Connections**. You will see the wireless Internet service you are using listed here. Right click your mouse over it and choose **Properties**. Finally, click on the **General** tab and untick the box which says **File and Printer Sharing for Microsoft Networks** (Fig. 9).

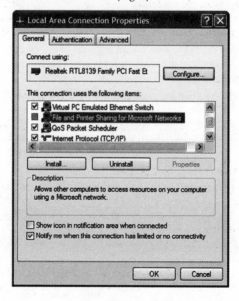

Fig. 9

Action 6

If you're using your laptop but don't need to use a nearby hotspot, switch off your wireless adapter completely to stop it receiving incoming signals. To do this, right click your mouse over the wireless network connection icon which you'll find at the bottom of your screen. Then select **Disable**.

Action 7

Buy software that helps secure your laptop from attacks when you're in a hotspot. Try SpotLock from jiwire. com, which also includes a built-in hotspot directory and personal firewall.

Section 10:
Getting Online Without a Hotspot

If you need to get online and there's no hotspot nearby, consider these two alternatives:

Surf Using Your Phone

The most flexible way to go wireless is to connect your laptop to a '3G' mobile phone service. 3G is offered by most major mobile phone companies and allows you to surf the web wherever you can pick up a 3G mobile phone signal. 3G mobile phones can also pick up standard mobile phone signals. Standard signals can be used to surf the web if you aren't in a 3G-signal area, but they are very slow. You can purchase a 3G data card from most of the major mobile phone networks.

Buy a 3G data card instead of a wireless PC card and place this in the PC card expansion slot on your laptop. Insert the software CD-ROM provided to complete set up.

There are a couple of problems with 3G. Firstly, it's slower than using a wireless hotspot, so whilst it's OK for e-mail or web surfing, it's not good for downloading files. Secondly, it's not cheap. That's why it's mostly used by business people.

Vodafone
vodafone.co.uk

T-Mobile
t-mobile.co.uk

Orange
orange.co.uk

Browse Offline
If you know you won't be near a hotspot but still want to visit a particular website at a later time, you can use an offline browser instead. Offline browsers capture web pages or entire websites and save them to your computer so you can look at them when you can't access the Internet. You'll need offline browser software to do this and you can download this online. Try the free HTTrack offline browser (httrack.com) or get a free trial of Teleport Pro at tenmax.com/teleport/pro.

Chapter Twelve:
The Best of Broadband

Essential Information

In the last few years, there has been a dramatic increase in the number of websites with exciting content especially for broadband users. Some websites are even aimed wholly at those with high-speed Internet connections. Find a great broadband website and you'll enjoy a much more engaging and interactive experience.

Here you'll find the very best broadband websites on the Internet, with the top twenty sites in each of a range of categories.

Section 1:
Education and Learning

Annenberg Media
learner.org
A US teaching channel with free access online.

BBC History Games
bbc.co.uk/history/games
These fun, animated games have an historical twist.

BBC Science Clips
bbc.co.uk/schools/scienceclips
This uses mini animations to explain the key areas of school science (suitable for all ages).

Broadwise

blueyonder.co.uk/tv

An educational TV channel that is designed especially for broadband users.

British Library

www.bl.uk

The *Turning the Pages* exhibition lets you read important manuscripts such as da Vinci's personal notebook, *Sketches by Leonardo* and *The Original Alice* by Lewis Carroll.

British Pathe

britishpathe.com

Gain access to over 3,500 hours of classic footage including news and social history.

Collect Britain

collectbritain.co.uk

Learn about Britain's cultural heritage from the 90,000 images and sounds from London's British Library.

Discovery Broadband

discoverybroadband.co.uk

You'll find the best clips from the Discovery science and nature TV channel.

GCSE Bitesize

bbc.co.uk/schools/gcsebitesize

Teenagers studying in the UK will find this website a great help when they need to revise for exams.

Google Print

print.google.com
Search on any topic or book title to view the pages of thousands of books.

History Channel

historychannel.com
Learn about the past with important clips of events that changed society and speeches from world leaders.

Hubble Site

hubblesite.org
Home of the Hubble Space Telescope, you can play games and watch video documentaries and images from space.

MSN Encarta

encarta.msn.com
Encyclopaedia with videos, maps, interactive features, 360-degree tours and sounds.

National Archives

www.nationalarchives.gov.uk
Important British historical documents can be viewed online – you can even research census details and trace your family tree.

Newsplayer

newsplayer.com
This has newsreel clips from the past hundred years online. A small annual subscription is required.

Research TV

www.research-tv.com

With video reports on the latest scientific studies, news and research, this also covers areas in society, business and health.

Smithsonian

smithsonian.org

Online exhibitions from a number of museums and galleries across the US.

Teachers' TV

www.teachers.tv

Contains hundreds of free videos for UK teachers but has equally useful advice for parents.

Theban Mapping Project

thebanmappingproject.com

Take an interactive journey with this project that catalogues finds from the Valley of the Kings.

Visual Thesaurus

visualthesaurus.com

For homework, brainstorming or creative writing, this dictionary and thesaurus uses mind mapping techniques to display results.

Section 2:
Fun and Inspiring

Arcade Arena

arcadearena.com

Filled with lots of classic arcade favourites. There are similar games at superarcade.com.

Guinness World Records

guinnessworldrecords.com

The Video Vault has fun record-breaking clips.

Brick Films

brickfilms.com

Amusing video shorts and spoofs created entirely with Lego bricks.

Cowboys and Engines

cowboysandengines.com

A 3D world where you can play games with other people.

Explore Mars

exploremarsnow.org

Take an online tour of the Red Planet.

Kontraband

kontraband.com

Sites listing TV ads, games, silly animations and 'viral' videos. Viral videos are short clips, usually passed around friends or office colleagues by e-mail, that sometimes gain a bit of a cult status online.

Metaboli

www.metaboli.co.uk
Download lots of top games for a monthly subscription.

MiniClip

miniclip.com
Hours of diversion with free online games.

Morphases

morphases.com
Entertaining face manipulation website.

My Space

myspace.com
Online community for meeting friends and sharing photos.

Outer Worlds

outerworlds.com
Chat online with your friends or make new ones in virtual
reality. You'll find similar worlds at habbohotel.com and
vzones.com.

Pirate Radio

pirateradio.com
Create your very own radio station and broadcast it on
the web.

Stupid Videos

stupidvideos.com
Thousands of silly and amusing video clips and
advertisements from around the world.

Talkin Toons

www.talkintoons.com

Entertain your friends with free full screen animated greetings cards.

Tate Online

tate.org.uk

Interactive entertainment from the Tate online galleries.

Technorati

technorati.com

Search millions of blogs and personal websites.

Blog Television

blogtelevision.net

Search for videos from millions of blogs and personal websites.

ViralBank

www.viralbank.com

Watch viral videos and pictures.

Yahoo! Widgets

widgets.yahoo.com

Contains software that gives you access to widgets – clever computer utilities written by people all over the world.

Yuks TV

yuks.tv

Watch video clips on music, film, games and comedy.

Section 3:
General Interest

BBC on this Day
bbc.co.uk/onthisday
Archive footage of what happened 'this day in history'.

BBC Video Nation
bbc.co.uk/videonation
Get an insight into the lives of the people of Britain by
watching hundreds of personal video diaries.

Chatshow Network
chatshow.net
Watch free video interviews with various celebrities.

Comedy 365
comedy365.co.uk
Popular source for comedy podcasts.

Community Channel
communitychannel.org
The UK's only TV channel for charities and good causes.

Download.com
download.com
The place to download free and paid for software. You'll
find more at tucows.com.

Go To Meeting
gotomeeting.com
Run an online meeting by allowing people to view your computer screen wherever they are in the world.

I Love the...
bbc.co.uk/ilove
Step back in time to your favourite decade.

Information TV
information.tv
Community information TV channel broadcasting free online.

Like Television
liketelevision.com
Watch classic old films and TV for a monthly subscription.

Moonfruit
moonfruit.com
Helps you to use simple templates and animations to create your own professional looking website.

NASA
www.nasa.gov/multimedia
See the latest pictures from space, watch NASA TV or visit the Astronaut Flight Lounge.

National Public Radio

npr.org

US public radio service that has interesting interviews and information on business, health, people and culture.

Pro: Fx

profx.us

Allows you to create an animated and interactive website.

Project Gutenberg

gutenberg.org

This is a database of over 17,000 eBooks you can download for free to your PC or handheld computer.

Putfile

putfile.com

This is a free place to store your photos and videos online.

QuickTime Guide

apple.com/quicktime/guide

Video content from Apple on entertainment, education and more.

Radio Lovers

radiolovers.com

A free website where you can download all the old radio series such as *Flash Gordon*, *Buck Rogers* and *Batman*.

Roland Collection
www.roland-collection.com
Over 600 free films about art.

Vid Net
vidnet.com
Free videos on the latest films, full-length music videos
plus updates on extreme sports and fashion.

Section 4:
Kids

Aardman
aardman.com
Watch animations, links and diversions from the studio
that created *Wallace and Gromit*.

Alfy
alfy.com
This US-based website has lots of games for you to play.

Animal Planet
animal.discovery.com
There's plenty of animal video news and entertainment
for everyone in the family.

CBBC
bbc.co.uk/cbbc
Website of the BBC TV channel for children, including
CBeebies for younger children at bbc.co.uk/cbeebies.

Cartoon Network

cartoonnetwork.com

Offers hours of diversion and hundreds of free online games.

Discovery Kids

discovery-kids.co.uk (or kids.discovery.com in the US)

Games, videos and fun from the Discovery TV channel.

Disney

disney.com

Great games and worlds to explore such as Disney Blast, Toontown and Kids Island. Some require you to pay a fee.

Fun Brain

funbrain.com

Cartoon-style website with interactive educational games.

Headline History

headlinehistory.co.uk

Teaches kids about British history in a fun, interactive way.

J. K. Rowling

www.jkrowling.com

Harry Potter fans young and old alike will enjoy this animated official website, written and updated by J. K. Rowling.

KiddoNet

kiddonet.com

Create your own online drawings, comics and virtual greeting cards.

Lego

lego.com

Provides games and ideas on what to do with your Lego bricks.

MSN Kidz

kidz.msn.com

You'll find games, quizzes and help with homework on this kid-friendly website.

Primary Games

primarygames.com

This has a range of games for younger kids, all of which are aimed at learning as you play.

Show Me

www.show.me.uk

Fun stuff for kids, from the UK's museums and galleries, including lots of educational games.

The Baby Channel

babychanneltv.com

You can watch hundreds of helpful videos on a variety of topics including child health, nutrition and pregnancy, although you will have to pay a small fee.

UniRoyal Fun Cup

funcup.com

This is an addictive racing game for kids of all ages.

Wonderville 3D

www.wonderville.ca

This is a virtual world designed to teach science to kids in a fun way.

Wonka

wonka.com

Enjoy sweet-themed fun and other games from Nestlé.

Yahooligans TV

yahooligans.yahoo.com/content/tv

TV clips, cartoons and more from the team at Yahoo!

Section 5:
Film

You'll find more online video and TV channels in Chapter Seven.

Academy Awards

oscar.com

Lets you watch backstage interviews and long, tearful acceptance speeches.

Apple Trailers

apple.com/trailers

This has all the latest films and videos.

Atom Films

atomfilms.com

Enjoy these short films for free, the genres include animation, comedy and drama.

Box Office 365

www.boxoffice365.com

Download films, comedy shows and music videos to watch on your computer for a small fee.

Cinequest

cinequestonline.org

Free DVD-quality feature films and short films.

Empire

empireonline.co.uk

The latest film trailers and news.

Film Festivals

filmfestivals.com

News and video from the red carpets of famous film festivals such as Berlin and Cannes.

Film Four

channel4.com/film

UK broadcaster presents film trailers plus a range of ten minute mini films and animations.

Flash TV

iwantmyflashtv.com

This online TV channel showcases short animated films.

Fun Broadcasts
funbroadcasts.com
Good quality video news from the world of music and entertainment.

IFilm
ifilm.com
Gain access to a variety of channels playing comedy shows, short films and the 100 most popular videos of the moment.

Internet Film Community
inetfilm.com
A database for filmmakers with some entertaining short films from new and up-and-coming directors.

Internet Movie Archive
archive.org/details/movies
Possibly the most comprehensive online public archive, it has thousands of free films and video shorts.

Like Television
liketelevision.com
Watch old cartoons and classic TV programmes for a small subscription fee.

MTV Movies
mtv.com/movies
This allows you to watch video interviews and behind-the-scenes footage. It also includes MTV Overdrive, a hybrid channel of TV and PC exclusively for broadband users.

Net Broadcaster

netbroadcaster.com

Have a look at film trailers, video shorts and mini films created by unknown film-makers.

Reel Classics

reelclassics.com

Old film clips and sound bites website run by a classic-film fanatic.

Screenplayer

screenplayer.com

This has over 1,000 hours of film related news footage and classic clips that you can access for a nominal subscription fee.

Student Film

studentfilms.com

Hosts short films from student film-makers for you to enjoy. Budding film-makers can upload their own films to the site for a small fee.

Sundance Film Festival

festival.sundance.org

All the news, video and archive footage from current and past festivals.

Section 6:
Music

You'll find more websites where you can download and buy music in Chapter Six.

AOL Music
music.aol.com
Free and regularly updated, this website has news, interviews, live events and full concerts.

BBC Music
bbc.co.uk/music
Contains all the best music from across the BBC.

Classic FM
classicfm.com
Listen to live classical music on your radio or watch Classic FM TV on the web.

Clipland
clipland.com
Search this database of over 16,000 music videos for your favourites.

E-Music Television
www.e-musictelevision.com
Live music video and Internet TV station.

Fab Channel
www.fabchannel.com
Music venues Paradiso and The Melkweg in Amsterdam record concerts and stream them online for you to watch.

Find Sounds
findsounds.com
This is ideal if you're looking for an unusual sound. Alternatively, you could try AltaVista audio search (altavista. com/audio).

Find Videos
findvideos.com
This has the latest and not so recent music videos.

Internet Music Archive
archive.org/details/audio
This website has thousands of music tracks and live concert recordings ready for you to download for free.

Lycos Music
music.lycos.com
Supplies a good choice of free music videos and links to TV clips and celebrity interviews.

Ministry of Sound
www.ministryofsound.com
Radio, games and web TV channel for fans of dance music.

MTV

mtv.com/music

Exclusive music video clips, radio, live interviews and events for you to enjoy.

Music.com

www.music.com/video

Watch a selection of current music videos, news and video interviews.

Music Brigade

www.musicbrigade.com

With thousands of full length music videos on demand, this site requires viewers to pay a monthly subscription but allows you to create playlists and watch all the latest videos.

NME

nme.com

Watch exclusive music and video tracks in the NME Media Player.

Rolling Stone

rollingstone.com

Read the latest music news, listen to free music and watch the latest videos.

Tiscali Sessions

tiscali.co.uk/music/sessions

Gives access to exclusive online performances as well as radio and music videos.

Video-C

video-c.co.uk

Watch the latest music videos for free.

Video TV

video.tv

Subscribe to this website to access thousands of full length music videos from before the 1970s to the present day.

VidZone

www.vidzone.tv

You will have to pay a monthly subscription to watch any of these high quality music videos from big name stars.

Section 7:
News and Sport

At the Races

attheraces.com

Live and archived footage of British, Irish and US horse racing for a monthly fee.

BBC News

bbc.co.uk/news

Up-to-the-minute news coverage, video and interactive features, including a regularly refreshed three-minute video news update.

BBC Parliament
bbc.co.uk/parliament
Live and archive coverage of the UK's House of Commons and House of Lords.

BBC Sport Player
bbc.co.uk/sport
Quick and easy access to the best sports-related news and clips of the day.

Bloomberg
bloomberg.com
Read the latest financial news for the US, Europe and Asia.

Broadsports
blueyonder.co.uk/tv
Provides access to a sports TV channel especially created for broadband.

CNN Video
cnn.com/video
Latest US and world news in video.

Eurosport
eurosport.com
Watch sports video news from across Europe, including news from the worlds of football, tennis and cycling.

F1 Play

f1play.com

Good video clips and information for F1 fans.

GolfSpan

golfspan.com

Watch hundreds of golf tutorials for an annual fee.

High TV

high.tv

The broadband TV channel for lovers of extreme sports, snow sports and surfing.

PGA European Tour

europeantour.com

Hundreds of free videos and radio news to keep up to date with the latest from golf's favourite European tournaments.

Pure World Cup

pureworldcup.com

Online access to World Cup action from 1958 to 1998.

Red Bull

redbullcopilot.com

Discover the excitement of Red Bull-sponsored races.

Reuters

reuters.com

The Reuters TV channel supplies excellent quality video news.

Revs TV

revs.tv

Good site for motor sports fans. A fee is necessary to watch each clip.

Sky News

sky.com/news

Free news video player; you can e-mail video feedback on the day's events to the studio.

Sky Sports Broadband

home.skysports.com/broadband

Top sporting action from one of the best sport TV networks for a monthly fee.

Sportal

www.sportal.com

Comprehensive website dedicated to the latest sports video and audio clips.

Wimbledon Plus

video.wimbledon.org

For a small annual fee get the latest tennis video and radio from The Championships, including full matches and archive footage.

Section 8:
Shopping and Home

Absolut
absolut.com
Lots of ideas and cocktail recipes for vodka lovers.

Ben Sherman
www.bensherman.co.uk
Interactive website for this famous menswear brand.

Dulux
www.dulux.com
With their Mouse Painter website you can try out home decorating and colour schemes, by painting your own virtual rooms.

Fashion TV
ftv.tv
Live web video channel for followers of fashion.

Food Network
foodnetwork.com/food/video_guide
Impress your family and friends with recipe and cookery ideas from this online cookery channel.

Free Foto
freefoto.com
A huge collection of over 75,000 free photos, perfect for work presentations, homework or home-made greeting cards.

Food Standards Agency

food.gov.uk

Games and interactive features to keep you informed and equally entertained.

Home and Garden Television

hgtv.com

US based video tips for DIY enthusiasts.

Ikea Kitchen Planner

ikea.com

The simple way to design a new kitchen online.

iVillage

ivillage.feedroom.com

News and features from this popular women's web portal.

Levi's

levi.com

Website for the famous jeans brand with extra features and downloads.

Living

living.com

US based online video magazine, updated monthly.

Nike

nike.com
Good for advice as well as shopping. Access other Nike sites such as nikefootball.com, nikerunning.com, and nikeid.nike.com, which allows you to buy your own customised shoes.

QVC

qvc.co.uk
Shopping channel which can also be watched live online. Visit qvc.com for the US version of the channel.

Royal Mail

www.royalmail.com
Personalise your UK stamps by uploading a picture to the Royal Mail website where they'll create special stamps for you (www.royalmail.com/smilers). Print them yourself with their SmartStamp system (www.royalmail.com/smartstamp).

The Hair Styler

thehairstyler.com
See your own photos with thousands of virtual hairstyles. You will have to pay a subscription.

UKTV Food

uktvfood.co.uk
Learn basic cooking techniques or search this database of over 1,000 video recipes and then watch famous chefs show you exactly how to make it.

UKTV Style

uktvstyle.co.uk

This website supplements the TV channel with a host of DIY ideas. It also includes uktvstylegardens.co.uk for those looking for gardening tips.

Vogue

vogue.co.uk

Watch exclusive fashion videos from designer shows.

Wrapsody

wrapsody.com

Upload your favourite photo and Wrapsody will create personalised wrapping paper for you.

Section 9:
Travel and Leisure

360 Travel Guide

360travelguide.com

Take 360-degree virtual tours of famous cities and landmarks.

4Car

channel4.com/4car

Video test-drive reports for car enthusiasts.

Adventure TV

adventuretv.com

Watch free videos about adventure travel.

BBC Languages

bbc.co.uk/languages
Learn to speak a new language with free web and video guides from the BBC.

BBC Weather Video Forecasts

bbc.co.uk/weather
Watch the weather report before you step outside.

Google Earth

earth.google.com
Allows you to view locations all over the world using satellite imagery.

Google Local

local.google.co.uk (or local.google.com in the US)
Simple 'zoomable' map for finding anything in your area.

Holiday TV

holiday-tv.com
Guides to destinations around the world.

London TV

visitlondon.com
Check out this video TV channel for what's on in London. It includes TubeGuru, an interactive guide to the London Underground.

Museum of Modern Art New York

moma.org

Excellent range of interactive online exhibitions.

National Geographic

nationalgeographic.com

Provides information on wildlife, travel and education plus many free video clips.

OAG

oag.com

Review all airport and air-travel queries including seating charts.

Online Travel Brochures

www.onlinetravelbrochures.com

Browse the pages of travel brochures from hundreds of UK tour operators.

Road MC

roadmc.com

Video tours of roads in Europe for real motorcycle fans.

Surfline

surfline.com

Surfers will love these video forecasts and live beach webcams.

Thomson
thomson.co.uk
Destination videos plus watch Thomson TV live for the
latest holiday deals.

Travelago
travelago.com
These video guides will help you decide where to go in
the world.

TravelBlog
travelblog.org
This is a travel guide by real people with destination
photos.

Virtually the World
virtually-theworld.com
Choose from over 14,000 360-degree virtual city tours
including many hotels.

What's on When
whatsonwhen.com/video
Plan your trips abroad with this selection of video
destination guides.

Jargon Busters

ad-hoc network
Describes the wireless connection of two or more computers (often laptops) by using wireless adapters. The network can be connected to the Internet by the addition of a suitably configured computer.

administrator account
Describes the type of user who logs on to Windows XP. The administrator is usually the computer's owner and has full access rights to install software, add or delete files.

ADSL
Asymmetric Digital Subscriber Line. The most common type of broadband delivered to your home via your telephone line.

blog
A series of updates (text, images or video) on a specific topic, regularly posted on a website.

clip
Refers to short video (or music) that you can watch or download from the Internet.

desktop
The screen you see on a computer when you first switch on and before opening any windows. Usually includes program icons and a recycle bin.

download
To copy information from the Internet on to a computer or other device.

emoticon
Graphic that represents emotion; used when instant messaging or sending e-mails.

Ethernet
Technology for connecting multiple computer devices together. Ethernet sockets can be found in modems and computers.

expansion slot
Socket on a computer that allows extra equipment (such as a wireless adapter) to be connected, which expands the capabilities of that computer.

firewall
Monitors and protects information passing to and from a computer via the Internet.

gigabyte
GB: indicates the size of a large file or storage space. Equivalent to 1,000 MB.

hotspot
Location where you can access a wireless Internet connection, either at home or outside, such as in a café.

infrastructure network

A wireless network of two or more computers that centres around a router, which is connected to the Internet.

icon

Image, symbol or graphic used in computing, which you can click on to perform an action.

kilobit

Kbps: measures the speed of a broadband service. 1,000 Kbps is equivalent to 1 Mb.

limited account

Describes the type of user who logs on to Windows XP. Limited account users have different login details to the owner of the computer and are restricted in how they can install software, add or delete files.

MAC

Also known as a 'MAC code' or 'MAC address'. Media Access Code: a unique serial number for wireless equipment used for identification when securing wireless networks; also used to describe a 'Migration Authorisation Code', required when switching from one broadband provider to another.

megabit

Mb: measures the speed of a broadband service. Equivalent to 1,000 Kbps.

megabyte
MB: indicates the size of a file or the computer disk space it takes up.

microfilter
Plugs into a home phone socket when using ADSL broadband to allow you to surf the Internet and make calls simultaneously.

modem
A device that connects your computer to the Internet via cable, telephone line or satellite.

mp3
The most common form of music file, it can be played on any computer or portable MP3 player.

network
Connects computers and other devices together to allow them to share the same files and Internet connection.

peer to peer
Or P2P for short; used to describe file-sharing networks that allow you to share files with other people using disk space on your computer and an Internet connection.

phishing
Process by which criminals and hackers attempt to acquire sensitive information (such as bank or credit card details) by distributing false e-mails and websites that appear to be from official organisations.

podcast

Regular feed of audio material to a computer or handheld device. Most often used to distribute the latest edition of a radio or music show.

Pop-up

Also pop-up window; describes a message or screen that appears on your computer.

router

A device to network several computers together, or to wirelessly transmit a broadband connection.

Service Pack

Essential software and security updates for your computer that are available to download from the Microsoft website.

SSID

Service Set Identifier; name given to identify a particular network.

stream

Refers to streaming media such as audio or video that is delivered on a website and watched at the same time. You won't be able to save a copy of the media to your computer and watch it again or at a later time.

spyware
Software that secretly monitors or alters your Internet activity without your prior permission; often downloaded in free software.

upload
To copy information from a computer (or other device) onto the Internet. Attaching a file to a webmail e-mail message is an example of uploading.

USB
Universal Serial Bus: a USB socket or port allows you to connect devices together, such as a modem and a computer.

vlogging
The process of creating a vlog or 'video log'. A video log is a series of updates on a specific topic, regularly posted on a website (also known as a blog) but predominantly in video format.

Voice-over-Internet Protocol
Also voice-over-IP: allows you to send and receive telephone calls using your computer.

webcam
Small video camera that allows you to send still and moving images over the Internet.

WEP
Wired Equivalent Privacy: a method of securing a wireless network, now superseded by WPA.

WPA
Wi-Fi Protected Access: an advanced system of securing a wireless network.

Wi-Fi
Wireless Fidelity: allows computers to connect to the Internet or each other without wires, by transmitting information using radio waves.

wireless adapter
A device that allows a computer to pick up a wireless Internet connection.

wizard
A mini computer program that guides you through complicated tasks such as networking or installing software.

The Beginner's Guide to eBay

Clare McCann

£4.99

ISBN: 1-84024-504-2
ISBN: 978-1-84024-504-2

Like the idea of eBay but too daunted to give it a try? Already using eBay but want to get more out of it?

This little book provides all the answers to the questions you were too afraid to ask, in a user-friendly, jargon-free way and – in true eBay style – for a bargain price.

Bursting with bite-sized nuggets of wisdom, this step-by-step guide for the uninitiated includes advice on everything from selling a picture frame to buying the car of your dreams. Whether you'd like to set up a stall or simply haggle at the world-famous online marketplace, this is the perfect companion for any budding 'eBayer'. What are you waiting for?

Clare McCann is the author of Succeed at Speed Dating and the founder of the popular website singlegirlabouttown.com.

**The Beginner's Guide to
Computers and the Internet**

Susan Holden and Matthew Francis

£5.99

ISBN: 1-84024-396-1

CPU, Intel, VDU, server, Megabyte, MHz, monitor, DVD...

Forget the technical jargon. This is a concise and down-to-earth
guide that will help you become computer literate – in your own
time and on your own terms. You can do it. Beginning with
the basics, *The Beginner's Guide to Computers* explains, in your
language, the useful terms and shortcuts that will enable you to
use a computer with confidence and competence.

www.summersdale.com